designing with plants

designing with plants

piet oudolf with noël kingsbury

conran
OCTOPUS

page 1 A grass, *Chasmanthium latifolium*, is silhouetted against the green of a garden. page 2 *Corydalis solida* subspecies *solida* pink form and a dark hellebore flourish together in the spring. page 3 (from left to right) *Eryngium alpinum* in full flower. *Helleborus croaticus* going to seed. *Veratrum nigrum* leaves emerging. this page (from left to right) Biennial *Eryngium giganteum* remains standing through the winter. The annual California poppy (*Eschscholzia californica*) has short-lived flowers, but can bloom for months and often self-seeds. *Echinacea purpurea* 'Rubinstern' is a long-lived perennial, making a fixed point in the border.

commissioning editor **Stuart Cooper**
senior editor **Helen Woodhall**
editorial assistant **Alexandra Kent**
copy editor **Sarah Sears**

designer **Amanda Lerwill**
typesetting **Olivia Norton**

picture research **Jessica Walton**
production **Sue Bayliss**
index **Helen Snaith**
botanical name corrections **Dr James Compton**

First published in 1999 by Conran Octopus Limited
a part of Octopus Publishing Group
2-4 Heron Quays, London E14 4JP
www.conran-octopus.co.uk
Reprinted in 2001, 2003

The right of Piet Oudolf and Noël Kingsbury to
be identified as the Authors of this Work has been
asserted by them in accordance with the Copyright,
Designs and Patents Act 1988

ISBN 1 84091 055 0

British Library Cataloguing-in-Publication Data
A catalogue record for this book is available
from the British Library

Colour Origination by Sang Choy International, Singapore.

Printed in China.

contents

introduction

Piet Oudolf has gained a reputation as one of the world's most forward-looking and inspired garden designers. This book aims to explain his work and make his method accessible to a wider public. Although Piet and his wife Anja are Dutch, and his work is a product of the Dutch relationship to landscape and to nature, his garden style can be easily applied to any region enjoying a similar climate, and there are also lessons to be learnt from his work that can be applied in most other climatic regions.

This book looks not only at planting design, but also discusses how we look at plants. While I have been getting to know Piet and his work, I have been encouraged to look anew at plants, particularly at times when they are supposed to be past their best. I have learnt to appreciate plants for the shapes of their flowerheads, not just for their colour, and to look at the balance of these shapes amid the patterns and textures created by their leaves and stems. I have found myself looking in a different way at plants in winter: not just at the most obviously striking forms and structures of seedheads, but at the subtle variety of brown tones of dead foliage, the contrasts between the dark masses of soggy leaves and the straw-like lightness of surrounding stems and the interplay between them. Much of this book is a re-evaluation of what we consider beautiful in the garden.

Piet Oudolf's work with plants concentrates on perennials rather than shrubs. Perennials (also known as herbaceous plants) die down every winter to re-emerge the following spring. While he uses shrubs in his work, it is perennials that are Piet's real passion and it is his use of perennials that makes his design style so distinctive. It is, he says, 'structure that is the most important aspect in designing with perennials', for these plants have a distinct structure that is unique to them and that is in a state of almost constant change over the course of the growing season. This book looks first at the different shapes to be found among perennials, and then at how they can be combined harmoniously in plantings, and how such plantings can be made part of the wider scheme of things in the garden. Thereafter the moods and emotions that can be created by perennial plantings are given close attention, and also how groups of perennials look at different times of year.

I first met Piet Oudolf in the summer of 1994, a year in which I had spent a lot of time travelling, primarily looking at garden design in a number of countries: the USA, Brazil, Germany and The Netherlands. I was keen to see what designers in other countries were doing because I was tired of the British garden-design scene, which

opposite left **An open border planting in Ingolstadt, southern Germany, illustrating a large-scale contemporary style.** opposite right **Traditional borders have always hugged a backdrop, usually a wall, which severely limits design possibilities.** above left **Rigidity is typical of the traditional over-manicured garden – there is little room for nature or spontaneity here.** above right **A deep understanding of plants, like these late-summer perennials, can lead you to create an exciting new look.**

seemed to me to be dominated by a backward-looking mentality. German parks, with their vast and romantic spreads of perennials, had been a revelation to me, as had many public plantings in The Netherlands, where extensive drifts of wild flowers introduced nature into urban environments. Piet's work, and the nursery which he runs with Anja, appealed to my love of plants while his gardens – a celebration of plants amidst the geometries of trimmed hedges and clipped shrubs – struck me as achieving an almost perfect balance.

Like many of his countrymen, Piet is very tall, with the weatherbeaten features of one who has spent a lot of time outside. He can take a while to get the measure of people the first time he meets them, but, once trusted, new colleagues and friends are treated to generous hospitality. Outwardly serious, he has an infectious smile and a good sense of humour, and he enjoys the company of others, but he generally prefers to work alone. He is immensely creative, but I rather have the feeling that he regards working with others as compromising this creativity. 'I don't need a discussion with other people, I know what I like; it is not worth arguing about.'

During the two years after I met Piet, I became acquainted with a whole circle of northern European garden and landscape designers, all concerned with bringing nature into urban environments and building a closer relationship between nature and the garden. The day I met Piet we spent a day in the company of Eva

below left **Wildflowers in the Rocky Mountains. North America has provided many of our best traditional herbaceous perennials.** below right **At Cowley Manor in Gloucestershire, England, Noël Kingsbury is attempting to apply the lessons of ecological planting in a country where traditional planting solutions are often favoured.**

Gustavsson, a Swedish landscape designer and academic, then doing research on planting design, and Henk Gerritsen, whose magical and entertaining 'Priona Garden' – created by Henk himself and his late partner Anton Schlepers – we all drove off to see. Soon afterwards I met Rob Leopold who, with his colleague Dick van der Burg, had spent much time since the mid-1970s assessing a range of annual flowers; these had been successfully marketed as seed, bringing a new lightness of touch to summer plantings. Later in the summer I visited more German gardens, and met Urs Walser, then director of the Hermanshof Garden at Weinheim in the Rhine valley, perhaps the most sophisticated of the German nature-inspired public gardens. Piet gains a lot of strength from being part of an informal movement, believing that shared thoughts usually achieve more than total isolation – a typically Dutch attitude, I believe. As he says, 'I want to be seen in a period ... you only make history with a group ... I need other people who have the same philosophy, otherwise I feel lost.'

Part of Piet's success as a garden designer has been his provision of a middle ground. His gardens and parks do contain formality, speaking of tradition and order, while a closer look reveals a lively recasting of classical geometries; his borders contain enough of the familiar to reassure the cautious and enough of the unfamiliar to entice novelty-seekers. As Henk Gerritsen says, 'his plants look wild, but his gardens do not.'

below left Before the white settlers came, the American prairie once covered huge areas with a rich flora, such as this *Echinacea angustifolia*; efforts are now being made to preserve the surviving fragments. below right The coast is a difficult environment for plants to grow in, yet the survivors have a startling beauty of their own.

Piet decided to train as a landscape gardener at the age of 25, after he had decided not to take over the restaurant and bar that was his family's business. Inevitably, his first influence was Mien Ruys. 'She was everywhere, the only garden designer in Holland who was talking about plants and plantings, the others just talked about design.' Her style was distinctly architectural, yet she also had a great interest in and appreciation of plants. Piet's own passion for plants was given a boost when he visited England for the first time in 1977. Among other places, he visited Hidcote and Alan Bloom's Dell Garden. 'I loved the atmosphere ... a kind of dreamland ... and plants I had never seen.'

During the earlier part of his career Piet worked in the densely populated western part of The Netherlands, near Haarlem. But in 1982, increasingly frustrated at not being able to obtain the plants he wanted to use in his design work, he and Anja decided to move to the more sparsely populated eastern province of Gelderland. There, north of Arnhem, just outside the village of Hummelo, they would spend several years converting an old farmhouse and establishing a nursery devoted to the cultivation of plants that they felt they needed. These years were hard but rewarding. The couple travelled widely to collect the plants that would become the seed corn of the future. In England, Beth Chatto was a great inspiration, as well as a source of plants. 'The way she ran the nursery inspired me ... and gave us the idea of setting up the nursery here,' Piet explains. From here and from many other British nurseries the Oudolfs bought geraniums, hellebores, lavateras and others. Certain German nurseries also proved to be a valuable source of plants, in particular that of Ernst Pagels, situated in the flat landscape of Ost Friesland, just across the border. Pagels had been a student of the influential nurseryman and writer Karl Foerster, whom Piet describes as 'my hero, for his unconventional way of looking at plants'.

It is Foerster, and his love of grasses and other plants uncorrupted by hybridization, who has been the single largest influence behind the northern European perennial movement. Piet and Anja also collected plants in the Balkans, a region especially rich in plant life; they found some particularly fine hellebores in Bosnia-Hercegovina just before war broke out there.

In 1984 the Oudolfs conducted an experiment which proved to be a watershed in the Dutch horticultural industry. They held an open day, which they advertised in the media, inviting other like-minded nurseries to come and sell plants. Nothing like it had been seen in The Netherlands before; people came and bought plants, while the nursery owners networked. Rob Leopold was struck by how generous Piet was 'and how inviting ... he has absolute authenticity and a flowing spontaneity, like a mountain stream.'

Part of the success of Piet as a designer and of the nursery he runs with Anja is the result of meticulous plant selection. From the species they have acquired he has selected forms that seem particularly gardenworthy. Some genera have been the focus of his special attention: asters, astrantias, monardas and, most recently, sanguisorbas. The selection and trialling process has often involved the kind of co-operation that is at the root of Dutch horticultural success. A local farmer is paid to grow seed-raised plants on an agricultural scale; the best are selected to be given names and propagated, and the remainder ploughed in. But raising colourful new cultivars has not really been at the core of Piet's work. His interest, as he explains, lies elsewhere:

above left Traditional borders have tended to rely on massed ranks of perennials organized mainly by reference to their flower colour, although here there are contrasting forms too. The yellow is *Achillea filipendulina*, the orange a helenium. above right Grasses are a major component of the modern garden, and their use is a clear distinction between traditional and contemporary styles, They remind us of nature and have a long season. Here varieties of miscanthus and molinia mingle.

'I want to use plants that gardeners have ignored before, such as astrantias, grasses and umbellifers (members of the Apiaceae – cow-parsley family), choosing those that have strong structures.'

Every garden makes a philosophical statement about the relationship between art and control on the one hand and nature and wildness on the other. The gardens that are the most successful in any particular historical period are those that reflect the particular point of balance between these two sides that is most in tune with the spirit of the times. Piet's gift lies in his ability to capture the current Zeitgeist. 'My biggest inspiration is nature. I do not want to copy it but to recreate the emotion,' says Piet. 'What I try to do is build an image of nature.' Talking about maintaining plantings, he says, 'You have to guide nature, or it gets out of hand, but you have to know exactly when to intervene. It is much more difficult than just clipping.' He is equally vehement about the need for thorough and ruthless plant selection as an essential part of this process: 'Having the best is essential. You have to work through masses of material and distill what you think you need. And I find now that I need less than I did.' The Oudolfs own garden acts as a trial site for the best new plants and new design ideas. Rob Leopold comments that 'his friends are occasionally horrified by how he can completely rip up parts of the garden and start again'; I have the impression too that nothing ever stays the same for very long there.

I believe that some of Piet's boldest design experiments have involved simply transforming the language of classical formality. He has combined box and yew in very formal simple patterns, for example, or twisted the axes of symmetry in the framework of his planting. Indeed, in his own garden he has created a vista that leads to the end of the garden, with beds along this main axis that are off-centre, and yew pillars planted to lead the eye down the axis in a zig-zag manner – so much more enticing than a traditional approach as it tempts the

viewer to look at more of the garden. On a rainy visit with a party of British visitors Sir Roy Strong called it 'wonky Baroque'. To complement these formal design modes, Piet has added another distinctive feature to modern garden design: mood and emotion. Eva Gustavsson believes that 'his strong emphasis on creating a straightforward emotional dimension, focusing not only on form but on the creation of strong atmospheres, goes beyond mere visual beauty.'

The Oudolfs'garden and nursery are a plant-lover's paradise: not only does it offer a wonderful opportunity to see – many unfamiliar – perennials growing in a garden setting, but then the plants are for sale too. Anja presides over the nursery. With her more extrovert personality, she is very much in her element dealing with customers and parties of visitors. It is Anja, too, who not only supervises the day-to-day running of the production side of the nursery but also organizes special events. She is an absolutely essential part of the Oudolf enterprise. The nursery itself is an experience in design. Plants of *Pyrus salicifolia* (silver pear) are clipped into pillar-like shapes (very rarely seen), while stock beds of perennials create a meadow-like effect. Some plants, notably the foxglove relative *Digitalis ferruginea*, and the spiky-looking *Eryngium giganteum* have self-seeded among paving slabs to create a forest of narrowly vertical flower spikes. Such spontaneity is an important part of the atmosphere.

Noël Kingsbury

below left and below Wild flowers are the inspiration for much of the work of contemporary garden designers. Here two details of a meadow in Slovakia in late summer illustrate the complexity and diversity of wildflower communities, the understanding of which is vitally important for successful planting design.

planting palettes

introduction

In the same way that a painter works with a palette of coloured pigments, so the garden designer can select what plants to use from a palette of plants. Traditionally, a plant's colour was its most important characteristic, but in this book plants will be examined in a different light for other qualities: firstly, for the shapes of their flower- and seedheads; then for their leaf shape and texture; and only then for colour.

Structure is the most important component in a successful planting; colour is important too, but it is a secondary consideration. If the forms and shapes of plants in a border work well together, and you choose plants that still resemble their wild ancestors, it is difficult to imagine an unharmonious colour combination arising. One reason for this is the proportion between the flowers and foliage of wild plants. Garden plants often have flowers that are large relative to the rest of the plant; so good proportions are lost and there is less green to buffer strong colours.

An understanding of the nature of the materials being used is fundamental to any artistic activity, and this chapter is dedicated to this understanding, looking at various categories of plant raw material. The next chapter looks at how they can be combined, but not by presenting hard-and-fast rules, which would only encourage an unimaginative way of working. Instead, basic principles are established, encouraging you to follow our example and exploit your own creativity in putting together plant combinations that prove harmonious and pleasing to you.

By seeking to base planting design on structure, it will become apparent that there is something more essential to the soul of plants than colour. Think of how many plants occur naturally in one colour but which, in the hands of skilful and enterprising nurserymen and plant breeders, are made available to the gardening public in so many more. It is much less common that highly bred hybrids differ radically from their wild ancestors in basic form. The form and structure of plants is more intrinsic to them than colour, and gardeners should be paying it more attention. Flower colour is with us for a relatively short season,

compared with the shape of a plant – with perennials from spring until winter. If you want to create plantings that evoke nature and provide a long-lasting season of interest, then you should concentrate on learning about plant form, and think of colour only as an exciting extra.

From when it first emerges from the ground in spring to when its rain-lashed and frost-scoured remains collapse sometime over the winter, a perennial has a form that is intrinsic and unique to itself. The sensitive gardener will observe that there are many more stages in the life of a perennial that are deserving of study and appreciation than simply the flowers – buds, unfurling leaves, seedheads, autumn foliage, winter's skeletal remains – although the dominant feature of most perennials remains the flowers and how they are arranged in a head – what botanists call the inflorescence.

The first part of this examination of the planting palette will look closely at these flowerheads and the characteristic forms that they take, forms that are often apparent even some time before the flowers actually emerge from their buds and forms that are, in many cases, strong sculptural features in the garden well after the flowers themselves have died and turned to seed. Often the core of a flower will expand and stiffen to form the seedhead, which will thus retain the essential shape of the flower, and will remain as a reminder of it, long after the flower itself has died.

Flowerheads come in a variety of forms, all of which have been adapted by nature to attract pollinating insects to the flowers, or, in the case of the grasses, to distribute the pollen on the wind. It is these forms that give flowering plants so much of their character, beyond the superficial layers of colour, and thus it is not surprising that plantings based on these forms will have a far greater durability and sense of balance than those which are planned purely around colour.

Botanists have various names which they use to classify the characteristic shapes of flowerheads (raceme, panicle, umbel etc.), but these often do not relate to their aesthetics, or how they work in the garden. Here flower shapes are grouped into rough categories according to their appearance. Sometimes there is confusion caused by our calling something a 'flower' when in fact it is a multiplicity of flowers making up a single solid head, as in a daisy. These so-called 'compound' flowerheads are particularly well adapted for insects, enabling them to browse large numbers of flowers for nectar without having to move any distance at all.

Foliage lasts longer than flowers, and has its own range of colours, shapes and textures, which the gardener would do well to pay plenty of attention to. Attractive and well-combined foliage is like a background to whatever performance the flowers put on – quite essential, in other words.

above **Flowers come in an extraordinary variety of colours, shapes and sizes. Often what we think of as one flower is in fact a complex head made up of hundreds, such as astrantia, achillea and helenium (2nd, 4th and 5th from left). Conversely, you can easily identify the individual flowers of *Epilobium angustifolium* var. *album* and *Perovskia atriplicifolia* (1st and 3rd from left), but it is still the whole that makes an impression.**

spires

Spires thrust our vision skywards, reminding us of other realms, connecting heaven and earth. Spire-shaped flowerheads add lift to the garden, severing its bonds with the earth. Spires contrast dramatically with other flowerheads and introduce a note of clarity amid other less clearly defined flower shapes or a mass of foliage. The form of a spire makes it a dominant visual element in any planting but they never look quite right on their own; a clump or loose gathering of spires is always more satisfactory.

Flower spires comprise a stem packed with flowers; the more tightly packed the flowers, the purer and cleaner the shape. Some have smaller spires branching out from one main one, all of them thrusting upwards at the same angle, to create a hazy forest of spires. Some have 'branches', where the side spikes grow outwards at an angle, which reduces their impact.

1 ***Digitalis parviflora*** Borne in midsummer, the tall, thin, elegant spires of this foxglove are an attractive mixture of browns, creams and yellows.

2 ***Verbena hastata*** Flowering in late summer, the whole plant points upwards.

3 ***Salvia* 'Dear Anja'** Named for Anja Oudolf, this new salvia variety bears broad spikes of flower in early summer.

4 ***Veronicastrum virginicum* var. *incarnatum*** Both the flowers and the supporting stems of veronicastrums thrust upwards, making them one of the most valuable of the new generation of perennials. This flowers in early summer.

5 *Epilobium angustifolium* var. *album* Related to the infamous 'fireweed', this pure white midsummer-flowering form is much less invasive.

6 *Salvia pratensis* 'Lapis Lazuli' Thrives on limestone soils and in sun. A pink form of a common European wildflower.

7 *Baptisia lactea* Grey-white flowers contrast with dark stems adding elegance to this American prairie perennial.

8 *Calamagrostis* x *acutiflora* 'Karl Foerster' The most upright of all the grasses, which bends in the wind, making it almost weatherproof.

9 *Lythrum* 'Stichflamme' Lythrums create impact by producing spires of flower in midsummer, often held in bunches.

10 *Thermopsis caroliniana* Loose yellow spikes in early summer.

11 *Agastache foeniculum* Another perennial that has spires in bunches, this flowers in midsummer, and is small enough to add stature to confined spaces.

12 *Persicaria amplexicaulis* 'Rosea' The plant itself forms a bulky, bushy shape, but the 'rat-tail' flower spikes have a lighter touch over a long late-summer period.

13 *Cimicifuga simplex* 'Atropurpurea' group – One of the few late-flowering perennials for shade, the gently bending spires of cimicifugas are ideal for any situation where they will never dry out.

buttons and globes

Buttons and balls are defined points, concentrated clusters of flowers tightly packed. They stand out against soft shapes like plumes or against veils of fine stems. In the summer they are often points of concentrated colour. In the winter they are often the only clear points in a planting, standing out against the soft and ill-defined decay of everything else as dark spots. In winter the number of buttons is increased, as certain other flowers, daisies in particular, lose their petals to be left with the round, central head. The effect that these shapes make is largely dependent upon how they are arranged. Some are set in whorls on upright stems, others in loose umbels, some stand alone atop stout stalks, others on scattered fine stems. Those arranged in more defined patterns will of course make a stronger impression. Their being spaced out on stems means that it is possible to see through clusters of buttons; they are effectively transparent, in the same way that groups of narrow stems are transparent.

1 **Sanguisorba officinalis** The tight dark red globes of this and other sanguisorba species are a distinctive feature of damp places in summer.

2 **Marrubium velutinum** The flowers of this early summer-flowering mint relative cluster in whorls around the stem. They are perhaps most noticeable in winter when everything else around them has collapsed.

3 **Trifolium rubens** Buttons with a soft edge on early summer-flowering clover. The leaves, each divided into three leaflets, provide interest before and after flowering.

4 *Echinops ritro* **'Veitch's Blue'** The globe thistle has a perfect spherical flower in midsummer, ripening to seedheads for the early part of winter.

5 *Salvia verticillata* **'Smouldering Torches'** Whorls of flower form globes in miniature.

6 *Phlomis tuberosa* **'Amazone'** An early summer-flowering perennial whose spires form into buttons when seen up close.

7 *Knautia macedonica* The dark red-pink flowers of this scabious are scattered through the border all summer.

8 *Monarda* **'Squaw'** Whorls of flower are characteristic of these mid- to late-summer-flowering perennials.

9 *Eryngium giganteum* The thistle-like bracts around the flowerheads of this biennial turn ghostly pale brown in autumn, emphasizing the tight central cone.

10 *Astrantia major* **'Roma'** Wearing a delicate ruff, the button heads of astrantias are an essential part of the garden in early to midsummer, in sun or light shade.

11 *Centaurea glastifolia* Brassy yellow heads make this mid-summer-flowering knapweed prominent.

12 *Allium hollandicum* **'Purple Sensation'** Ornamental garlics often have flowers in spectacular spherical heads, which stand for some time as seedheads after the flowers have finished.

plumes

Plumes are a soft form, intermediate between spires and umbels. They too are composed of a myriad of tiny individual flowers, but arranged in a looser, fluffier, often more transparent way. Being somewhat intermediate they act to connect the shape of spires and umbels in the upper reaches of the border. Their vague fluffy quality is particularly effective *en masse*, evoking in particular the flowering of many marsh plants, like reeds and meadowsweet. The way that some plumes tend to be unidirectional is a particularly attractive feature, as all the breeze will direct all the plumes in a planting to point the same way, for example the seedheads of the miscanthus grass. Too many bold or clearly defined shapes in a border can create the impression of fussiness or be almost overstimulating. The presence of less clearly defined forms like plumes acts like the softness of the colour pink, as a linking form, making it easy to bring together the stronger shapes.

1 **_Filipendula rubra_ 'Venusta'**
A beautiful delicate pink form of a wet prairie perennial, among the softest of all flower/shape combinations, flowering in early to midsummer on tall stems. It thrives in moist soil, but also does well in average garden soils.

2 **_Solidago_ 'Goldenmosa'** Goldenrods combine strong yellows with unusual swept flowerhead shapes. There are now new tidy varieties available, so there is no excuse for not using them in the end-of-season border. Wild species show a surprising number of different flowerhead shapes, many of which have a lightness of

touch that is a welcome contrast to the heavy-looking, and rather aggressively spreading, older varieties.

3 **Thalictrum lucidum** This has relatively tight plumes of soft yellow flowers in early summer, which stand above dark green divided foliage.

4 **Aralia californica** Spherical clumps of flower gathered together in plumes above bold and dramatic foliage in late summer. This is a large plant and needs space in order to look its best.

5 **Rodgersia 'Die Anmutige'** Among the most dominant of plumes, these stand boldly upright, yet they have a soft appearance. Early to midsummer-flowering, for wet and lightly shaded places.

6 **Thalictrum aquilegiifolium var. album** These fluffy rounded plumes are very distinct in early summer, on any non-drying soils. It is one of the earliest flowering tall perennials, making it a very valuable plant to contrast with the lower clump shades characteristic of most early species.

7 **Persicaria polymorpha** White plumes on branches that radiate out all summer long on this bulky shrublike perennial, which has been one of the best new introductions of recent years.

8 **Calamagrostis brachytricha** Plumes of soft mauve-tinged grey make this grass an ideal companion to the more defined shapes that you generally find in later season plantings.

umbels

Umbels are the familiar upturned bowl shapes of many common wildflowers and 'weeds'. These are the flowers of wild, unkempt places, many of them not regarded as garden flowers. But once we have set aside the shibboleth that a plant has to be colourful to be allowed into the garden, we can begin to appreciate the beauty of these flowers. Umbels are, in a way, the opposite to spires, their gently rounded shapes counterbalancing the energy of the sky-seeking spires. Composed of hundreds, or even thousands, of minute individual flowers, they often have a soft and gentle look. Many have flower clusters that form highly complex patterns, often umbels within umbels. The most important plants with umbel flowers are those of the umbellifer family, which play an important part in many wild habitats. This, along with the soft creams and off-whites of their flowers means that when used in the garden they lend a look of gentle naturalism.

1 ***Foeniculum vulgare* 'Giant Bronze'** The herb fennel has flat-topped dull yellow umbels in early summer set among finely divided foliage.

2 ***Smyrnium perfoliatum*** Tiny, delicate umbels sit in expansive ruffs. Flowering in early summer before the leaves emerge, this is a plant of shade.

3 ***Angelica gigas*** Flowering in mid-summer, these dark red flowerheads attract attention wherever they are placed.

4 ***Phlox paniculata* var. *alba*** Rounded heads of pure white illuminate the midsummer garden in sun or light shade.

5 *Sedum* **'Stardust'** A cultivar with broad, flat-topped umbels.

6 *Lychnis chalcedonica* var. *albiflora* Relatively large flowers form a tight rounded umbel. Flowering in early summer.

7 *Phlox paniculata* **'Düsterlohe'** A lilac-rose phlox hybrid.

8 *Angelica* **'Vicar's Mead'** Heads of compound umbels stand above dark foliage on a classic umbelliferous perennial. Like many umbellifers it tends to die after flowering, but usually sets seed.

9 *Sedum telephium* subsp. *ruprechtii* The sedums provide some of the most valuable late-season umbels, often favoured by butterflies.

10 *Eupatorium purpureum* subsp. *maculatum* **'Atropurpureum'** Attracting droves of butterflies, the pink heads of the 'Joe Pye weed' top a majestically large late-summer perennial.

11 *Molopospermum peloponnesiacum* One of the most impressive of the umbellifers, its stature leads it to dominate its surroundings.

12 *Chaerophyllum hirsutum* **'Roseum'** Fluffy umbels in late spring or early summer evoke hedgerows and banks of wildflowers.

13 *Achillea* **'Terracotta'** The umbels of many achilleas fade delightfully to different colours as they age.

daisies

Daisies remind us of the sun, not just because of their shape but also because they are so often found in sunny places: meadows, fields and prairies. Plants with daisy flowers tend to flower from midsummer onwards too, which makes them even more strongly associated with the sun and the heat. There is something undeniably optimistic about them. Daisies are like even more concentrated versions of umbels, masses of tiny flowers so closely packed together that they are usually taken to be a single flower, but with the outer flowers having ray-like petals, creating the characteristic daisy appearance. The central and the outside petals are often different colours, which can give them a particularly striking appearance. After flowering the outer petals generally drop off, leaving buttons behind, which are often very persistent.

1 *Echinacea purpurea* 'Green Edge'
Echinaceas have some of the largest and boldest of daisy flowers, the petals tending to reflex away from the central cone. In flower, in midsummer, they look at their best just as they are beginning to go over, introducing a note almost of decadence.

2 *Echinacea purpurea* 'Rubinstern'
A more conventionally coloured cultivar of echinacea than 'Green Edge'.

3 *Rudbeckia fulgida* 'Goldsturm'
Flowering from midsummer to early autumn, this is one of several dark-eyed yellow rudbeckias that keep the feeling of summer going whatever the weather. Unlike many later-flowering perennials they tend to be compact, making them very versatile.

4 *Aster* **'Herfstweelde'** Flowering until quite late in autumn this is a free-flowering variety, one of many asters that make the end of the year a potentially very colourful time.

5 *Aster* **'Octoberlight'** With smaller flowers than 'Herfstweelde', this is also a very late-flowering variety, which makes it very useful for those days when the first frosts have killed any half-hardy plants and other late perennials are being buffeted by wind and rain. Like most asters it prefers average to moist soil and sun.

6 *Inula magnifica* **'Sonnenstrahl'** All inulas have exceptionally fine outer filaments, but this midsummer-flowering variety is unique in having them so long that they hang down.

7 *Helenium* **'Rubinzwerg'** The heleniums offer the russet shades of autumn in flower form. Although it is the outer petals that initially attract the eye, it is worth paying attention to the contrasting colour of the central cone too.

8 *Aster amellus* **'Sonora'** A striking mauve-blue cultivar of an aster species that is more tolerant of drier soils than most; indeed it is only really happy on light or limestone soils, disliking clay or ground that is overmoist in winter.

9 *Silphium perfoliatum* The yellow flowers of the 'prairie docks' stand aloft on stems that may reach three metres or more, in late summer. The large leathery leaves are striking too.

screens and curtains

Plants do not always have solid shapes; some form a network of stems, leaves and flowers that allow you to see right through them. Think of how you can see through the flower stems of grass. Transparent plants are mostly air, and their loose growth creates another perspective as you look through them to the plants growing behind. The very narrowest spire shapes may be transparent, especially when used *en masse*, or the branching stems of umbellifers. Conventional planting, with its massed ranks of planting, misses out on this special quality. But transparency can be overdone; it can destroy patterns if too many such plants are used, drawing attention away from the real concept. The trick is to create the impression that it is everywhere, when in fact it is not. Think of such insubstantial plants as the raw material for screens and curtains in the garden, allowing you to see through or past them to get some idea of what is hidden behind. Used in this way, they can generate highly effective combinations of colour and form as well as an atmosphere of mystery and romance.

1 **Stipa gigantea** This grass, with its oat-like flower and seedheads on far-flung branches is the archetypal 'transparent' plant, at once both large and insubstantial. It is a strong feature of the garden from early summer to midwinter.

2 **Thalictrum polygamum** The plumes of this early summer-flowering perennial are scattered on tall thin stems, making it possible to 'see through' the plant. After flowering it maintains its stature and interest for a considerable time.

3 *Miscanthus sinensis* 'Graziella' alongside a helenium. The narrow flower- and seedheads of this miscanthus cultivar are thin enough to subtly blend in with neighbouring flowers. Both flower in late summer to early autumn.

4 *Molinia caerulea* 'Transparent' is a 2m- (6ft-) tall, late summer-flowering grass whose heads are amazingly light, creating a softly insubstantial haze, perfect for catching autumn dew.

5 *Sanguisorba tenuifolia* 'Alba' The narrow, pendent flowerheads of this sanguisorba catch the light, especially when in front of a dark background, making a curtain-like effect.

6 *Thalictrum delavayi* Close up, the flowers of thalictrums appear quite different to how they do normally, but the feeling of airy delicacy remains.

7 *Sanguisorba officinalis* The button flowers of this perennial are so widely scattered on a network of narrow stems that the plant can be seen through, to whatever is behind, allowing strikingly beautiful combinations to be built up. By nature a marsh plant, this will thrive in the garden anywhere that does not experience summer drought in full sun.

8 *Foeniculum vulgare* 'Giant Bronze' The narrow leaves and sparse umbels of a young fennel plant create a screen effect, making visible what can be seen behind. Older plants may become considerably more bulky and opaque.

shape

Shape is fundamental to the way that we see the world. In the garden, leaf shapes have a particularly strong effect on us, especially in the short or middle distance, an effect which is often accentuated by distinctive or attractive colouring or texture. Given that flowers are only a relatively temporary phenomenon for most plants, we would do well to pay more attention to the value of foliage in the garden. Plants with large or bold leaves create a different impression to that created by those with small leaves or leaves that are divided into many small leaflets. The former stand out, becoming resting points for the eye as it sweeps across a planting, whereas the latter tend to sink into the background. Waterside or other moist environments are particularly rich in large- and bold-leaved plants, but if nothing but dramatic foliage is used the effect can be fussy and overstimulating. Small-leaved plants do not emphasize their presence from afar, yet closer to they may hold our attention if they are of high-enough quality. Linear foliage, like that of grasses or irises, is a contrast to that of most perennials and creates variation and interest. Anything with a leaf shape that is distinctly different to that of most surrounding plants can be repeated to develop a sense of rhythm in a planting.

1 **Asarum canadense** Like many other woodland ground-covering plants, asarums have attractive dark, glossy leaves, a complement to low-growing and subtle-flowered shade-loving plants. There are a great many species, showing a huge range of silver- and grey-splashed heart-shaped leaves, making them ideal for cool confined spaces.

2 *Euphorbia nicaeensis* The young foliage of euphorbias can be attractively glaucous. This species, along with many others, starts its growth early in the year, new buds slowly unfurling the season's complement of leaves, a welcome sign of new life.

3 *Epimedium grandiflorum* Invaluable in shady situations as ground cover, epimediums form dense clumps of heart-shaped leaves, often flushed pink or bronze in spring.

4 *Stachys byzantinus* 'Big Ears' The neatly shaped, densely woolly leaves of this low-growing evergreen perennial have interesting texture, colour and shape.

5 *Hosta* 'Halcyon' The bold leaves of quality hostas, such as this, have a sense of quiet majesty, their relatively uncomplicated leaf shapes acting as resting points for the eye.

6 *Cynara cardunculus* Related to the globe artichoke, this large perennial starts to make growth early in the year which makes it especially valuable, although it does need full sun and lots of space.

7 *Pulmonaria longifolia* hybrid Almost evergreen, the pulmonarias are hard-working plants that deserve to be grown for their attractive silver-splashed leaves almost as much as for their early spring pink or blue flowers. Hugging the ground in light shade, they provide interest through the summer, long after most woodland plants have finished flowering.

texture

Texture is a particularly underrated aspect of plants. Yet looking for it often reaps rewards, especially if you study leaves which are just unfurling in spring, when the pleating and quilting that is characteristic of some foliage is at its most marked. Although some textures stand out in all surroundings, particularly if they are glossy and catch the light, generally how much we appreciate the texture of foliage depends upon how close we are to the plant. Plants with fine textures are most easily appreciated when they are situated at the front of the border or in an intimate setting. Here they can be an accompaniment to those flowers that also demand closer attention. Soft light, or at least situations where light does not strike the plants full on, is particularly important for the full appreciation of texture. In addition, plants from shady or moist environments are more likely to have leaves with an interesting texture – notably ferns.

1 **Potentilla peduncularis** It is remarkable how close examination of plants reveals beauties that are not normally appreciated. This is especially true of young foliage. The hairy leaves of some potentillas are especially attractive as they unfurl.

2 **Hosta 'Blue Angel'** The colour and texture of hosta leaves varies greatly from hybrid to hybrid. Those like 'Blue Angel' that have pleated leaves are especially attractive, the veining creating a feeling of quality – luxuriance almost. Tightly wrapped hosta leaves open to pleats and finally expand into large heart shapes, with a quilted appearance. They need cool, moist places and are easily damaged by slugs.

3 *Helianthus grosseserratus* Many perennials have deeply textured leaves so that each species has a subtly distinct appearance, even when it is not in flower. Like most of the perennial sunflowers, this one has big yellow flowers and loves full sun.

4 *Miscanthus sinensis* 'Pünktchen' Anything with 'linear' leaves creates a contrast with surrounding perennials. This ornamental grass has an unusual banding on the leaves which creates a strong impression of visual texture, even from far away. Full sun is important for miscanthus to be successful, otherwise they are tolerant plants.

5 *Heuchera micrantha* var. *diversifolia* 'Palace Purple' The heucheras are noted for a special attribute, where the colouring of some of the leaves deepens the effect of their texture. The clump-forming habit of dark-leaved heucheras make them useful plants to dot among others for continuity. They require sunny spots or those with only light shade.

6 *Veratrum nigrum* has some of the most extravagantly pleated foliage of all perennials. Here it emerges from the shoot which has thrust up through the spring soil. It needs moist well-drained soil.

7 *Rodgersia podophylla* 'Saarbrücken' Rodgersias have some of the most dramatically textured of all garden leaves, with deep ridges and furrows enhancing their distinct colouring and large size. Rodgersias only develop their full glory in moist places, and do not mind light shade. They also need plenty of horizontal space.

hot

Colours towards the warmer end of the spectrum become psychologically more dynamic, drawing attention to themselves in a way that cooler colours do not. This is why they need to be used with caution – as brief splashes of alarm among colour harmonies. Some gardeners, however, gain great pleasure from planting 'hot' borders, mixing yellows with purple or bronze foliage, although often they will find that there is only a somewhat restricted range of plants available, particularly as regards high-quality reds. Red, however, is the first colour to disappear at dusk, and 'red borders' can present a depressing and sombre spectacle at this time of day. Dark reds also speak less strongly of warning than paler reds or oranges; they evoke a more mysterious atmosphere, making them good companions for other flowers of more unusual and enigmatic colouring.

1 *Tulipa sprengeri* One of many bulbs that provide the brilliant dabs of colour that help to make spring a vibrant experience. A hot sunny place with no competing vegetation is important if tulips are to flower every year.

2 *Papaver orientale* 'Leuchtfeuer' Notably short-lived, poppy flowers are as delicate as tissue paper, but they are usually strongly coloured. The papaver is long lived and self-seeding.

3 *Clematis viticella* variety Bearing blood-red flowers in midsummer, this clematis is useful for decorating walls or to run through shrubs that flowered earlier in the season.

4 *Paeonia* Paeonies have a short flowering season, but the size and often exquisite colouring of their flower heads more than make up for this. This variety is a saturated red; there are also good pink shades available.

5 *Imperata cylindrica* 'Rubra' Given its shape, size and scale, the Japanese blood grass provides spectacular colour, especially when backlit. It is not an easy plant, however, needing full sun and a moist but not waterlogged situation, and preferably acid soil. Note that the colour starts in the tips of the shoots in spring and gradually suffuses throughout the plant as the summer progresses.

6 *Lilium* x *dalhansonii* The reflexed flowers of 'turkscap' lilies are unusual as well as colourful, and are always elegantly displayed on upright stems. Sun and fertile soil will ensure many years flowering.

7 *Lobelia* 'Fan Tiefrot' Lobelias provide some of the most intense colours for the mid- to late summer period. Naturally solitary plants, they can be used to provide isolated splashes of colour in the border. They are especially effective later in the season when all about them are beginning to look a little jaded.

8 *Dicentra* 'Bacchanal' With a long flowering season, this small and rather delicate-looking dicentra in fact offers an intense colour for more intimate spaces in the garden. It does best in light shade and dislikes drought. If the plant is happy, large clumps can be formed.

cool

Blue is a 'cool' colour which looks best in the reduced, cool light of early morning or evening. It is also a recessive colour, so that blue flowers and objects appear further away than they really are, a very useful characteristic because it enables you to give border plantings a feeling of great depth.

True blue flowers are relatively rare; most are spring rather than summer flowers. In fact, most 'blue' flowers contain some red, which means that pleasing harmonies can be created with purples and violets, which contain more substantial quantities of red. In contrast, blues with a very grey or metallic quality are particularly unusual and require very careful placing in order that their qualities can be truly appreciated.

1 *Aconitum carmichaelii* Wilsonii **Group** One of many blue aconitums, which tend to flower in midsummer, and often look best if grouped in clumps.

2 *Campanula latifolia* 'Gloaming' Campanulas are an unusual lilac blue, making them one of the most valuable sources of blue-mauves in the garden.

3 *Amsonia tabernaemontana* var. *salicifolia* A drought-tolerant early summer-flowering perennial whose flowers are an unusual shade of steely blue.

4 *Clematis integrifolia* A herbaceous clematis that also produces attractive fluffy seedheads that add visual and textural interest later in the season. It forms a stout spreading plant with distinctive divided leaves, a noticeable feature even before it starts to flower in mid- to late summer.

Pink is one of the most common flower colours, especially in early summer. It is also one of the easiest to use, and acts as a superb linking colour, making connections between other stronger shades. It works particularly well in climates where the skies are often grey and clouded and the colour of the light is soft. For this reason it is all too easy for pink to be over-used: too much pink and the effect can be too sweet, cloying and without character or substance. There are many different pinks, which has a bearing on how they work in combination with other colours: some contain traces of blue, for instance, which are soft and harmonious, while strong magenta pinks can be among the most aggressive of all colours.

1 ***Sanguisorba stipulata*** The softness of the creamy white flowers is accentuated by the fluffy appearance of this midsummer-flowering species.

2 ***Papaver orientale*** 'Kleine Tänzerin' In contrast to the strong colours of many poppies, this variety is a most delicate shade of pink, though it also has dark and alluring eyes.

3 ***Salvia pratensis*** 'Lapis Lazuli' A pink salvia that mixes well with the more usual blues and mauves of this important group of early summer-flowering drought-tolerant perennials.

4 ***Lavatera cachemiriana*** The delicate pink flowers which last over a long period in summer make this a useful border plant, and also one that provides a valuable link between stronger-coloured flowers.

sombre

These are unusual colours, darker versions of more familiar tones. They attract attention not for their intrinsic nature but because they are unusual, an effect that can be enhanced by combining them with other colours. These colours have depth, and a sense of mystery, and when combined with pale colours can create startling and sophisticated effects.

Only a few plants naturally have very dark flowers, but many produce the occasional one which has – these can then be propagated by nurseries. The same applies to dark foliage. Only those with marked gothic tendencies might want to plant a whole collections of such dark-leaved and dark-flowered plants together. The rest of us will only use them for occasional highlights, or in places where they can stop the curious visitor in their tracks – for an element of surprise they are invaluable.

1 **Astrantia major** 'Claret' type
Astrantias have flowers in a variety of sombre and subtle colours through the midsummer period and are versatile plants.

2 **Cimicifuga simplex Atropurpurea Group**. Although not flowering until relatively late, the dark leaves of this cimicifuga are of value from spring onwards.

3 **Hemerocallis** 'Little Grapette'
Daylilies display an enormous range of unusual flower colours, including several very dark tones. They flower from early to mid summer.

4 **Cirsium rivulare** 'Atropurpureum'
Flowering intermittently over a long season, this large thistle relative has flowers in an attractive and rarely seen shade of red.

The colour that is not a colour. Brown, like green, is omnipresent in the garden and there is a danger that we forget it. There are few brown flowers; it is a colour more likely to be found in grasses and dead foliage. The end of the year is the most rewarding time for brown; there are myriad shades and a soft light that brings out the best in them. Look for the pinky browns of some grass seedheads, the yellowy ones of some dead leaves and stems and the really dark browns that certain leaves turn after a hard frost. Remember too that the earth is brown, and how many variations there are: red, yellow and black are the main additional colours. Areas of bare earth in the garden are unnatural, and often undesirable; better to have them partially clothed by the earthy shades of foliage so that soil and foliage can mirror each other.

1 *Miscanthus sinensis* 'Malepartus' Many of the miscanthus grasses have earthy shades, but can paradoxically be simultaneously lit up by low sunlight.

2 *Echinacea purpurea* Once they have finished, flowers go to seed, their colours reflecting that of the earth.

3 *Eupatorium purpureum* 'Atropurpureum' As the off-pink flowers fade, they take on dull earthy tones, with the leaves turning the colour of dark prairie soil after a frost.

4 *Veratrum nigrum* Very dark flowers are unusual, and have a strange fascination. In the case of this veratrum, they are enhanced by the elegant form of the plant.

designing schemes

introduction

A successful plant combination relies primarily on shapes: the shapes of flowers or flowerheads of species that complement each other if they flower together, or flower, seedhead and plant shapes that combine well.

The shapes of leaves and their texture play a part too in a plant combination, as does colour. Colour, though, is only an added extra. A good planting should have enough variety of shape to look interesting in a black-and-white photograph – looking at it again in colour should add another dimension, but a secondary one. Colour has much more to do with the overall mood of the planting. Finally there is the dimension of time to consider, as perennials and grasses have such a dynamic way of growing, changing form dramatically as the year proceeds. In contrast to many shrubs, which keep the same shape all year round, and which are often similar in shape to each other, each perennial has a characteristic shape that is unique to it, and which changes almost constantly as the plant grows, flowers and eventually dies back.

Different aspects of a plant may play a key role in a combination at different times of the year. The elegant and distinctive leaves of sanguisorbas look attractive from spring until midsummer, when the tight, globular flowerheads take over as the prominent feature. Even after the flowers have died the seedheads have a part to play; in autumn they form clearly defined points among a mass of dying and decaying vegetation. So at each stage in both its life and death the plant has a decorative part to play in the border.

Using the plant palette as a guide, it is possible to bring together plants of different shapes, the aim being to create a combination that evokes a sense of balance and harmony. Combining different shapes and textures generates a creative tension that keeps both the eye and the imagination interested. However, it is also sometimes possible to bring together several plants of the same shape. Two sets of spires could be planted together, for example: the blue spires of delphiniums and the pure white of *Epilobium angustifolium* var. *album*. In this way the eye is forced to acknowledge both the similarities and the differences between the two plants.

Creating plant combinations is a very personal process; there are no fixed rules about mixing particular numbers of shapes from the planting palette. These kinds of rules only make a garden formulaic and lifeless. It is important that you look at these selections as an inspiration, not as a set of instructions, and that you make combinations that feel right for you.

Experienced gardeners often make changes to their gardens, in such a way that every winter sees a few plants being dug up and moved around. Less committed or less confident gardeners might find this surprising, but it is all part of the evolving process of gardening. Often plants are moved because the gardener is unhappy with a particular combination of plants, or has thought of an improvement, or perhaps because the plant is not thriving in its current position. In any of these cases it is best to make a note of the desired changes during the summer, so that plants can be moved in the winter when they are dormant and therefore can be moved with little harm being done to them. One of the marvellous things about perennials is how easily most of them can be moved around like this, although it is not suggested that it is done every year.

Such moving of plants around is part of the process of learning about plant combinations, and every year can bring new insights and inspirations which need to be incorporated into the garden if it is to be satisfying. Looking at how plants combine in other gardens, whether they are private gardens or open to the public, is an important way to find out about plant combinations, as is nature itself. Even if we do not want a particular wild plant in our gardens, we might still be able to learn something that we can make use of at home, from the way that it grows in relation to other plants.

The relationship between colour and form

1 Related shapes + related colours

The sum can be greater than the sum of the parts (1+1=3); the subtle interplay between two or more very similar shapes and colours can create a powerful impression.

2 Different shapes + related colours

Colour gardeners, like Nori and Sandra Pope of Hadspen House in Somerset, England, create colour-themed borders where plants with flowers of various shapes but of very similar colours are brought together.

3 Related shapes + different colours

This can be very successful, although how much contrast is considered harmonious is a matter of personal taste.

4 Different shapes + different colours

There is a danger that there will be too much contrast. The eye may be overstimulated, and there may be no common ground. This is only a suggestion to be cautious, however, as even outrageous contrasts may work!

above **Designing plantings involves composing with everything that plants can offer: flower colour and shape, foliage tone and texture, the overall shape of plants, and the qualities they have when they have died back. Every plant has a particular quality which the gardener** needs to understand in order to be able to use it effectively. Some have a quality that is most effective *en masse*, others are better combined intimately with others. Perennials tend to have an inherent strong shape, but some shrubs are more effective if they are cut into shape.

combining forms

above *Knautia macedonica* pink form and *Allium sphaerocephalon* flowerheads occupy more or less the same amount of space in early to mid summer, but present a different face to the world; one tight and compact, the other softer at the edges.

right *Lavandula intermedia* 'Grosso' and *Eryngium ebracteatum* are examples of two plants of an approximately similiar shape contrasting hard definition with a softer edge.

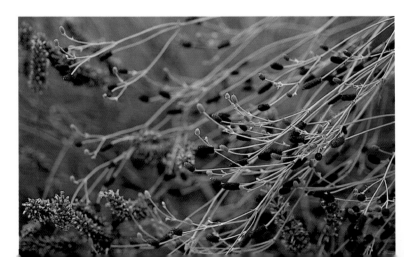

The planting palette, based largely on the shapes and characteristics of flowerheads and stems, is the basis for producing a harmonious planting. Quite how the plants are combined is up to you; the following is only a guideline, an introduction to general principles.

Think first about the effect that is created by a planting in which all the flowers have the same form: all spires, all buttons, or all daisies. However attractive the colours may be, it would look somewhat monotonous, as would a combination of plants with only two shapes. Think about wild-flower meadows you have seen, and ask yourself about why they have the visual impact that they do. One of the reasons for their beauty is the variety of flower shapes they embrace: the mixture of thistles and daisies, the umbels of many common wildflowers, the buttons of scabious and buttercup, the spires of verbascum and digitalis. It is an ordered evocation of this variety that I seek to create in my perennial plantings.

Spires and umbels are the two most striking opposites, the one vertical and heaven-seeking, the other horizontal, the flatness bent by a slight curvature serving to remind us of the shape of the earth itself. The most effective wildflower spectacles and garden plantings often have the combination of these two shapes as a central dynamic. Between

spires and umbels are plumes which can act as a filling element in the top layer of flowerheads, linking the two stronger forms. Plumes can be symmetrical, or asymmetrical. The latter are particularly effective when blown by the wind, all the plumes pointing in the same direction, as the flowers and seedheads of reeds in a wetland.

Buttons and daisies form sharp points of definition among the larger features of spires, umbels and plumes. As a general rule, they tend to be

At first glance it is difficult to tell that these are two different plants, so similar is their colouring. This is a combination for midsummer, and will thrive in full sun.

1 *Echinacea purpurea* 'Green Edge' just on the point of opening its big daisy flowers, the petals of which reflex slightly.

2 The harder and spikier *Eryngium giganteum*. As the echinacea flowers die, they drop their petals to leave the central cone to turn into a seedhead. The eryngium though only changes colour, to a straw-like tone, which is very persistent through the winter.

1   The ball-shaped flowerheads of *Echinops sphaerocephalus*, their edges backlit, are the dominant feature among less clearly defined shapes.

2   *Phlomis tuberosa* has distinct whorled flowerheads which echo those of the echinops and which have the advantage of winter persistence.

3   *Verbena hastata* has tiny flowers that are packed into small spikes which are an effective counterpoint to the hard

definition of the echinops.

4   *Selinum wallichianum* has umbels whose delicacy acts as a buffer between a variety of harder, sharper shapes.

5   *Veronicastrum virginicum* 'Fascination' has a strongly vertical and linear quality which moves the eye heavenward, balanced by the leaves which radiate from the stem in a remarkably neat way.

This is a planting for midsummer which will thrive in full sun.

1   *Sanguisorba officinalis* has flowerheads in an unusually dark tone which more than makes up for their small size. They contrast strikingly with the echinacea.

2   *Echinacea purpurea* has flowerheads of a more conventional colour and a bold shape and size. The combination of the two plants works well on two different levels: firstly the two plants are connected visually

by the shapes of their flower heads – in the way the central zone of the echinacea mirrors the bobbles of the sanguisorba. Secondly, they are connected by their colours – by the fact that they bear some relationship to each other. This combination looks good from mid- to late summer, and will thrive in a sunny position, in average to slightly moist soil.

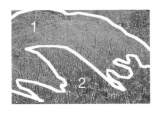

1   The stout daisy shapes of *Echinacea purpurea* 'Augustkönigin' dominate this planting.
2   In texture, the vertical plumes of *Astilbe chinensis* var. taquetii 'Purpurlanze' are a gentle fluffy contrast to the echinacea, and in shape provide an effective perpendicular contrast to the horizontal thrust of the echinacea.

3   *Scutellaria incana* is a filler plant, whose less clearly defined flowerheads help buffer the strong shape of the echinacea and the contrasting astilbe. All three form a harmonious contrast and colour combination. An early to mid summer planting for full sun, and average to moist soil. The astilbe and the scutellaria will tolerate some shade.

1   The grass *Molinia caerulea* 'Transparent' has myriad tiny flower- and seedheads which trap both light and dew, looking like mist or frozen gossamer from the distance. Generally upright, they can flop over when wet, as has happened here.
2   *Persicaria amplexicaulis* 'Rosea' forms a round clump from which numerous flower spikes emerge, here making a clear contrast to the wispy nature of the grass.

This planting works well from summer through to late autumn. It should be planted in full sun, in average to moist soil.

found on lower-growing plants than spires and plumes. Sometimes they are isolated hard dots; at other times, when they occur in large heads, they may form whole constellations, standing out against the foliage behind. Buttons and daisies are often found scattered in large heads, the interlinking stems having a transparent quality. In contrast to this transparency, the most clearly defined buttons are vital for the sense of definition they bring to plantings, something for the eye to catch hold of.

The transparent quality of screens and curtains is important for creating plant combinations as it allows us both to see something and to see through it, enabling us to build up layers of planting. Imagine a plant with such a transparent quality. We can see through it to some spires behind, but because the spires themselves are not a solid wall, we can see other flower and leaf shapes as well. By contrast, density is the opposite, an opaque block to vision. Density anchors and structures the whole planting. Sometimes it makes us pause, at other times it hides other plants from our vision, making us move around to see what is behind them, making us engage physically with the border in order to appreciate it.

Bold leaves stand out and act as punctuation, resting places for the eye, helping to develop rhythm. A planting without any bold leaves can dissolve into a morass of detail, and will lack any kind of structure. Linear leaves, like those of grasses, irises and hemerocallis, along with other linear forms, such as the upright stems of *Veronicastrum virginicum*, also help to add structure and variation in pattern. Different leaf textures add yet another dimension to a planting: glossy, matt, pleated or furry leaves are a source of constant variation, which the eye savours in ever-increasing detail as we look closer at a planting.

combining colours

Colour is an essential part in the development of a particular mood in the garden. Often, however, people are unadventurous because they believe that there are right ways and wrong ways to use colour. No colour can be wrong by itself; it depends on how it is used. In fact, no combinations are really wrong either, just unfashionable.

Colour themes are most effective when they are used in small areas within a wider context, so that they are just one theme among many. A limited number of blue-mauve flowers may be grouped together, but chosen so that they all have very different flower shapes. In this way you will be better able to appreciate the contrasting forms as much as the colour. Grouping closely related colours and using harmonies of related colours, such as pinks, reds, white and cream, or lavenders, mauves and blues, takes this idea a stage further. Using complementary colours takes it further still, where strong contrasts are orchestrated between colours that are effectively opposites, such as yellow and violet. By then, however, there will be so much contrast, on top of contrasts in foliage, texture and plant shape, that the effect may lack harmony.

Sometimes an awareness of plant shapes and textures allows you to do things that traditional dogma on combinings colour would suggest might not work effectively. For example, most of us believe that pink and yellow 'do not work', which is very often true, but if two plants that have the same form are put together, such as *Echinacea purpurea* and varieties of helenium, both of which have daisy-like flowers with a ray of petals arranged around a central cone, the very fact that the former is purple-pink and the latter yellow or orange makes the combination more attractive. One reason why colour is such an issue for many gardeners is because of the variety of plants available; there are just so many hybrids with showy flowers quite out of proportion with the size of the plant, particularly among annuals and half-hardy species. If we are aiming to create gardens that are inspired by nature, however, this is not so much of a problem, because wild plants, or those that are close to their wild ancestors, have flowers that are in a natural proportion with their leaves and stems. There is also a higher proportion of green to flower than there is in highly developed garden hybrids, and green is a 'buffer colour' that serves to separate and moderate the effects of stronger colours. There is simply much less scope for unharmonious colour combinations when working with plants that are close to nature.

opposite above **Monarda** 'Talud' stands out against the straw tones of *Deschampsia cespitosa* 'Goldschleier'. opposite centre **Salvia** x *sylvestris* 'Mainacht' and *Viola cornuta* have similar colours but contrasting shapes – an effective combination. opposite below Pink and orange are not always a happy marriage, but soft orange **Achillea** 'Terracotta' and dull lilac *Origanum laevigatum* 'Herrenhausen' work well together.

opposite top **The pink** *Lobelia* **'Eulalia Berridge' mixes well with dark purple** *Angelica gigas,* **red** *Helenium* **'Rubinzwerg' and** *Molinia caerulea* **'Transparent'.**
opposite centre **White and the rarer black (***Iris chrysographes* **black form), as well as green, are useful connecting colours.**
opposite below *Lobelia* **'Eulalia Berridge also combines well with** *Eupatorium purpureum* **'Atropurpureum'.** below **Pinks can range from the flesh tones of** *Eupatorium maculatum* **to the bright pinks of** *Thalictrum delavayi* **'Hewitt's Double'.**

connecting and dominant colours

It is often useful to think about colours in two groups: those which are strong, like hot reds and yellows, and those which are more subtle, like pinks, violets and blues. The former group of colours can all too easily dominate a planting if a harmonious balance is not carefully planned. Red, for example, is perhaps most effectively used occasionally, to develop a sense of rhythm in a planting; if used carefully, the points of red provided by individual plants or groups of plants will act as punctuation marks among areas of softer, less-defined colour. Red also adds a sense of dynamism and energy. Dark reds are particularly effective for creating a sense of rhythm, and fit in with other colours better than crimsons and scarlets, partly because they stand out less. If a colour that is

creating rhythm is too strong it takes over, so that it becomes difficult to appreciate other aspects of the planting, such as form and texture.

Many yellows are very dominant, like the strong tones of many of the daisy family (*Asteraceae/Compositae*), or plants such as helianthus or rudbeckia. Sometimes indeed the amount of yellow at this time of year can be overwhelming – which makes perennials with paler yellow flowers, such as verbesina, very welcome. Yet you can incorporate these colours in the border quite subtly if you choose plants whose flower shape alters the way the colour is seen: varieties of helenium, for example, where the various, more muted, colours of the central cone soften the impact of the yellow.

It is easier to use larger quantities of soft colours, like pink and lavender, or cool blues. Pink, in particular, is very useful, because it connects well with other colours, and

can act as an intermediary: between white and blue, for example, blue and purple, or red and white. Fortunately, there is an abundance of pink flowers available, especially in early summer.

Blue is a recessive colour; it sinks backwards and can be used to give depth when used at the back or end of a border. It has the opposite effect to strong colours such as magenta, which when used in the distance serve to make that distance seem shorter. Blue mixes well and you can take advantage of the range of blues and the varying degrees of depth that they create to build variations on a theme: by blending different *Salvia nemorosa* hybrids, for example. Another role blue can play is in lightening and giving depth to dark colour combinations, as when salvias, nepetas or blue phloxes are mixed with purples.

mysterious colours

I think of purples, dark reds and violets as being 'mysterious' colours. Purples can be used with strong colours like reds and yellows to calm them down. This enables you to bring these colours together comfortably in a planting, whereas in traditional bedding schemes, where there are few, if any, intermediate colours, they produce harsh contrasts and an extremely hard effect.

You will find that dark colours like purple work in combinations that you might initially think would be unsatisfactory: *Cimicifuga simplex* 'Atropurpurea' with dark-flowered astrantia varieties like *Astrantia major* 'Claret', for example. The dark purple-brown leaves and the deep red together create a brooding presence in a planting that is far greater than that produced by either of the two standing alone, illustrating how dark colours like deep blood-reds and purples serve to 'pull you in', creating a sense of depth and mystery.

structure & filler plants

The planting palette is about form and structure, shape and texture. Some plants have outspoken personalities; their forms make them dominate others, and it is they that will always dominate a planting visually. Think about the yellow-brown foxglove relative *Digitalis parviflora* and a hardy geranium: the digitalis is more striking to look at because its narrow spike of flowers makes a stronger statement than the formless, hummocky geranium.

Some plants have clearly defined, strong structures: many of the larger grasses, for example, with their long stems and distinct flowerheads; echinops with its big, dramatically cut leaves and globe-like flowers; or the rosettes of hostas. Others, which may lack a clear shape, may still have flowers or other characteristics that make them stand out: species of potentilla or the common grey-leaved *Stachys byzantina*, which lack any clear shape of

their own, tend to creep around other plants, often filling in gaps left between plants with a less flexible mode of growth. So, there are structure plants and filler plants. Filler plants are vital, as many structural plants do not mesh together well, and in any case too much structure can have an overstimulating effect. As a general rule, the proportion of structure plants to fillers should be 3 to 1. Filler plants are particularly useful at the front of the border. Most are grown for their flowers, some for their foliage; others may be chosen for the speed with which they develop and cover ground.

Some of the forms outlined in the planting palette – spires and umbels, for example – are so strong that they automatically define the plants as structural. But filler plants may also be counted as daisies or buttons in the planting palette, depending on their flower shapes.

right **When autumn fades the colours in the border, the strong forms of structural plants become more and more important.** *Miscanthus sinensis* **'Roland' dominates the background with the purple flowers of** *Vernonia crinita* **'Mammuth' in front of it and** *Helenium* **'Flammendes Käthchen' to the left. The foreground is dominated by** *Persicaria amplexicaulis* **'Rosea', bold when in growth but very much a filler plant as it collapses with the first hard frost. To the left of this is the grass** *Calamagrostis brachytricha.*

It may be useful to think of structural plants and fillers as representing two ends of a spectrum, with most plants coming somewhere between the two. Persicaria, for example, comes in the middle. It has bold leaves that are large enough to make the plant stand out clearly and flowers forming rat-tail spikes that are obvious too, yet its overall shape is not strong. When grown on its own, it becomes a rounded hummock, and among other plants of a similar size it tends to shape itself around them, like the dough in a baking tray.

Whereas structural plants stay neat, or at least distinctive, after they have finished flowering, filler plants tend to look messy, often because they lose their distinctive shape. Think how quickly the neat hemispheres of a hardy geranium turn into a sprawling mass of collapsed stems once the flowers have died. A lavender, on the other hand, or one of the bushy perennial salvias, like S. nemorosa, keeps its characteristic shape when the flowering season is over.

Some structural plants keep their shape for longer than others. The echinops, for example, has leaves that tend to die early in the autumn, and its globe-shaped flowerheads turn quickly to seed and fall apart, and yet it looks good for most of the season, its bold leaves being

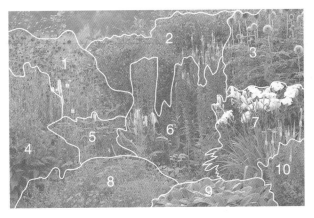

Filler plants for late spring

Aconitum napellus

Amsonia

Geraniums, especially *G. phaeum, G. endressii, G. x oxonianum, G. pratense, G. psilostemon, G. traversii, G.* 'Brookside', *G.* 'Patricia'

Geum

Lamium orvala

Lunaria rediviva

Papaver orientale

Nepetas, especially *N. x faassenii, N. racemosa, N.r.* 'Walker's Low'

1 *Monarda* 'Squaw' has distinct button flowers that create impact long after its flowering season is over.

2 *Helenium* 'Flammendes Käthchen', which is structural over a shorter season, and *Veronicastrum virginicum* 'Inspiration'.

3 *Echinops sphaerocephalus* has unique ball-shaped heads.

4 *Persicaria amplexicaulis* 'Rosea' is a a bulky filler plant, collapsing with the first frosts.

5 *Achillea* 'Feuerland' is useful for filling space at low levels, with long-lasting flower heads.

6 *Lobelia vedrariensis* has clear structure in flower, but little character afterwards and *Sanguisorba canadensis* has a strongly structural flower shape.

7 *Hemerocallis* 'Gentle Shepherd' is a useful filler plant.

8 *Dianthus amurensis* is a low level filler at the front.

9 *Stachys byzantina* 'Big Ears' is a neat long season filler.

10. *Nepeta racemosa* 'Walker's Low' is another low-level filler.

a strong feature for months before it flowers. Reliability is an extremely important consideration when you are choosing structural plants; they need to be absolutely hardy and not prone to pest problems, or sensitive to sudden changes in the weather, otherwise you may end up with large gaps in a border mid-way through the season. You should resist the temptation to use some of the increasing numbers of exotic-looking but not reliable hardy species that are now becoming available, unless you are prepared for the extra effort their failure may cause.

In shaded areas where there are often few structural plants, structure is provided by shrubs or tree-trunks, filler plants should be used in drifts.

1   *Stipa calamagrostis* has a light fluffy aspect which adds a romantic touch to the late summer garden. Despite its looks, its seedheads persist well through the winter. Its floppy but elegant habit give it something of the character of both a structural and a filler plant.
2   *Monarda* 'Purple Ann' echoes the colour of the eupatorium in a stronger form, and its persistent whorled flower clusters are also a strong structural element.
3   *Calamagrostis brachytricha* combines a clear shape with an attractive fuzziness over a long late summer to winter season.
4   *Artemisia lactiflora* Guizhou group has plume-shaped flowerheads that spring up from dark foliage. While in flower it is a good structure plant, but less so after it has finished.
5   The majestic shape of *Eupatorium purpureum* 'Atropurpureum' dominates this grouping. Relatively inconspicuous until it produces its butterfly-attracting umbel flowerheads in mid- to late summer, it remains an important structural element in winter. This is a planting for late summer in full sun, in average to moist soil.

above These plants maintain a strong structure long after flowering, often all through the winter: they include the tall airy grass *Stipa gigantea* and the umbels of *Sedum* 'Matrona'.

The gradient between structural and filler plants

*This diagram positions a number of perennials on a gradient
running from least to most structural.
It also demonstrates how this can vary at different times of the year.*

FILLER PLANTS

↑

The most amorphous, low-growing shapes, i.e., extreme
filler plants,becoming even more shapeless after flowering:
Geranium x *oxonianum* 'Rose Clair'
Campanula poscharskyana
Saponaria x *lempergii* 'Max Frei'
Viola cornuta

|

Less amorphous, somewhat taller filler plants that tend
to become more amorphous after flowering:
Centranthus ruber
Knautia macedonica
Euphorbia dulcis 'Chameleon'

|

Intermediate plants, many of them becoming
strongly structural after flowering:
Eryngium giganteum
Thalictrum aquilegiifolium
Phlomis russeliana
Salvia nemorosa
Sedum telephium

|

Intermediate plants, tall and structural in flower, but
becoming markedly less structural after flowering:
Hemerocallis hybrids
Macleaya cordata
Molinia caerulea
Phlox paniculata
Persicaria amplexicaulis

|

The strongest shapes, i.e., taller, very structural
plants that maintain their structure even through the winter:
Cimicifuga simplex
Filipendula rubra
Eupatorium purpureum
Miscanthus sinensis
Monarda hybrids
Veronicastrum virginicum

↓

STRUCTURE PLANTS

selecting and using filler plants

Our admiration of the sculptural qualities of certain plants or the magnificence of big perennials should not make us think that the so-called filler plants play a secondary role, for without their supporting role borders will be too rich and there will be too much competition between strong personalities. Filler plants may produce very attractive flowers over a long season, or they may flower or look good at a different season to the structural plants. They also have a practical function, because in covering the ground they minimize the amount of bare ground that can be colonized by weed seedlings.

You should choose filler plants that are strong-growing and reliable, but not invasive. When you select them you should have a good idea of how wide and how fast they will spread. Most will only spread a limited amount, and usually not much after the third year, but some, such as varieties of lamium or some types of geranium, can keep on spreading further, which may not be desirable.

Early-season filler plants, such as the hardy geraniums, provide useful colour at a time before the larger, and later-flowering, plants of the border begin their display. Others can be used later in the season, filling gaps around spring-flowering plants. This is especially useful in shaded areas: a herbaceous clematis like C. x *jouiniana* 'Praecox' is a good example because it can act as ground cover over pretty large areas.

left *Stachys byzantina* 'Big Ears' may be a low-level filler plant in a border, where its silvery leaves are useful for plugging gaps between taller perennials, but it can be very effectively used in mass plantings such as this one with *Hemerocallis* 'Pardon Me'. above *Centranthus ruber* is an early to midsummer flowering perennial which performs the filler function well in any sunny situation; here it spills over between border and path. The grass behind it is *Stipa gigantea*, whose stems form a transparent mass, effective from early summer through to mid-winter. To the left is *Thalictrum polygamum.*

Bushy filler plants

Late-spring and early-summer flowering

Aconitum napellus

Geraniums, especially:
   G. phaeum, G. endressii,
   G. x oxonianum, G. pratense,
   G. psilostemon, G. traversii
   G. 'Patricia', G. 'Brookside'

Geum rivale

Lamium orvala

Lunaria rediviva

Nepetas, especially:
   N. x faasenii, N. racemosa,
   N. r. 'Walker's Low'

Paeonia species

Papaver orientale

Mid- to late-summer flowering

Aster lateriflorus

Ceratostigma species

Diascia species

Geraniums, especially:
   G. wlassovianum
   G. procurrens
   G. 'Dilys'

Gypsophila paniculata

Persicaria amplexicaulis

Saponaria x lempergii 'Max Frei'

Filler plants for foliage

Hakonechloa macra

Hemerocallis species and cultivars

Heuchera species

Hosta species and cultivars

Larger, shrubby filler plants

Caryopteris subspecies

Indigofera subspecies

Lespedeza subspecies

leaf shape and texture

Many structural plants and filler plants may have leaves that are of special interest for part of the year because of their shape, their colour or their physical or visual texture. These qualities are especially important in shaded areas where the number of plants that flower after early summer is greatly reduced, so the presence of heucheras, the distinctive palmate (hand-shaped) leaves of hellebores or glossy clumps of epimediums and asarums is particularly welcome.

Plants with bold leaves have already been considered (see pages 32–33), but leaves have many other qualities. Colour is becoming increasingly popular, with more and more cultivars being selected for their variegated, purple or yellow leaves. Occasional purple-foliage filler plants like *Euphorbia dulcis* 'Chameleon' or *Anthriscus sylvestris* 'Ravenswing' are a good way of heightening contrast, especially early in the year among later-flowering perennials, while those with yellow foliage often look diseased, and if used at all should be planted sparingly and never close to each other. Of course, personal taste varies but these colours can often look very artificial. Silver foliage looks more natural; indeed, it is usually the outcome of a plant's adaption to a dry climate.

Texture is a quality that becomes apparent at close quarters: the wonderfully pleated leaves of *Veratrum nigrum*, for example, or the rough textures of many salvia species. Plants with interesting textures need to be positioned in situations where they will be noticed, giving those who are not used to looking in detail at plants an opportunity to do so.

using grasses

The use of grasses in gardens exemplifies the inspiration of nature. Long eschewed by gardeners, they are now at the forefront of planting design as increasing numbers of people begin to recognize their qualities, especially their reliability, long season of interest and tolerance of a wide range of different, and often difficult, environments.

Grasses possess special qualities that do not always fit into the conventional conception of the garden. They have a lightness of touch, a subtlety and an elegance that just does not look right next to hybrid roses, double flowers and bedding plants – the denizens of the traditional 'tidy' garden. Yet grasses are essential companions for the perennials that make up the contemporary garden.

Given their relative novelty, it is not surprising that many gardeners do not know quite what to do with them, and start timidly with the small, coloured foliage species, most of which are in fact sedges rather than true grasses: *Carex testacea* with its golden-bronze foliage, for example. Really to exploit the creative potential of grasses means being bolder and learning to appreciate qualities that previously might not have been considered important.

One such is the degree to which having grasses in the garden evokes a closeness to nature. Most open, wild environments are dominated by grasses; they form the foundation of many of the wild plant communities whose flowers are often the initial focus of our explorations of wild spaces. Simply having grasses in the garden immediately relates the garden to nature, forming a link with the surroundings if it is a country garden, or a timely reminder of wild places if it is in the city.

This effect of creating the feeling of nature is especially true of the medium-sized and larger grasses. Of the large number of varieties of miscanthus, *M. sinensis* is the most useful, with its neat, tall flower spikes that ripen to seedheads that remain a strong feature throughout the winter, with the asymmetrical look characteristic of reeds. Perhaps it is the most important border plant of the winter; combining delicacy with bulk, its seedheads are clearly defined even in the morning mist or the drizzle of a wet day. Species of molinia, calamagrostis and deschampsia are smaller than most of the miscanthus but are also reminiscent of wild places – grasses that could be encountered on walks along the woodland edge, perhaps, across moorland or through mountain meadows.

The ability of grasses to respond to light makes them invaluable, particularly in the winter, their subtle browns and yellows almost glowing in low winter sunlight while their seedheads can seem to catch the sunbeams. The soft texture and quiet colouring of many grasses, combined with the fact that they do not have colourful flowers, makes them a useful element in any planting,

Grasses with flower- and seedheads that move in the smallest breath of air

Stipa calamagrostis
Molinia caerulea arundinacea cultivars
Panicum virgatum
Stipa gigantea
Stipa pennata
Stipa pulcherrima

above right *Eryngium planum* 'Blaukappe' and *Stipa barbata* make an unusual combination.

right *Stipa pulcherrima* is one of the most spectacular of grasses with 30cm (1ft) long awns that sway and move in the slightest breeze. Its season is short, however, and it is not as easy as most grasses, needing dry soils and a lack of competition. It is best combined with other drought-tolerant plants, especially low-growing ones, for example in gravel gardens.

providing a rest for the eye, an opportunity to concentrate on some of the other, perhaps less dominant or demanding visual features.

· Not only do grasses catch light from the air but they also respond very gracefully to the actual movement of the air itself. Indeed, some grasses are never still for more than a moment; either bending backwards in the breeze, or bowing down under stronger gusts of wind, they constantly bring another dimension to the border: the dynamic of movement.

The ability to capture light and movement are two special characteristics of many of the stipa grasses whose appearance is slightly less familiar to anyone who comes from cool, temperate climates. Their flower- and seed-heads have a particularly soft appearance which perfectly complements the harder and more clearly defined shapes of most flowers.

All grasses have linear leaves which stand in striking contrast to the leaf shapes of most perennials, and they generally have a clearly defined habit, with radiating leaves

or stems rising upwards from the base. This linearity and habit again makes a most useful contrast to the habit of most perennials, making grasses a useful punctuation mark in the border.

Wonderful plants though grasses are, it is possible (as with everything in life) to have too much of a good thing. Placing different species of grass right next to each other is not generally visually pleasing; in particular, it seems that the different patterns of the radiating linearities of their leaves clash. Nor, on the whole, do they make successful companions for roses. There is too much of a contradiction between the intensely gardenesque nature of most roses and the wild beauty of grasses.

left Grasses and perennials are at their best in the late summer and early autumn. Here *Miscanthus sinensis* 'Zwergelefant' towers above perennials.

right In a dry gravel garden *Stipa turkestanica* waves above *Sedum telephium* 'Munstead Red' and *Eryngium proteiflorum,* showing how grasses can bring a touch of lightness and movement to situations dominated by rather solid clump-forming plants like the sedum.

Grasses that make a dominant feature:

in large spaces

Arundo donax

Calamagrostis x acutiflora 'Karl Foerster'

Cortaderia subspecies

Miscanthus floridulus

Miscanthus sinensis hybrids such as
  M. s. 'Gewitterwolke'
  M. s. 'Gracillimus'
  M. s. 'Grosse Fontäne'
  M. s. 'Kleine Fontäne'
  M. s. 'Kleine Silberspinne'
  M. s. 'Kaskade'
  M. s. 'Malepartus'
  M. s. 'Morning Light'
  M. s. 'Pünktchen'
  M. s. 'Richard Hansen'
  M. s. 'Roland'
  M. s. 'Silberturm'
  M. s. 'Undine'

Molinia caerulea arundinacea cultivars

Saccharum ravennae

Stipa gigantea

in small spaces

Calamagrostis brachytricha

Carex pendula (invasive, so wild areas only)

Chionochloa rubra

Hakonechloa macra

Helictotrichon sempervirens

Miscanthus sinensis 'Flamingo'

Molinia caerulea species and cultivars

Panicum virgatum and cultivars

Pennisetum species and cultivars

Sesleria nitida

Spodiopogon sibiricus

Stipa arundinacea

Stipa calamagrostis

Stipa pulcherrima

Grasses with seasonal interest

Grasses which have distinct autumn or early winter colour

Calamagrostis brachytricha

Andropogon gerardii

Deschampsia cespitosa cultivars

Hakonechloa macra

Miscanthus sinensis cultivars e.g.
  M. s. 'Afrika', *M. s.* 'Ghana'
  M. s. 'Flammenmeer'

Molinia caerulea cultivars

Panicum virgatum cultivars

Schizachyrium scoparium

Spodiopogon sibiricus

Sporobolus heterolepis

Grasses with distinct winter shape

Calamagrostis brachytricha

Calamagrostis x acutiflora 'Karl Foerster'

Deschampsia cespitosa

Miscanthus sinensis cultivars

Molinia caerulea (not *arundinacea* cultivars),

Panicum virgatum cultivars

Pennisetum alopecuroides

Sporobolus heterolepis

left *Angelica gigas* adds its mysterious purple tones to a midsummer medley of perennials. To the right is *Sanguisorba officinalis* Asiatic form.

below left Fennel (*Foeniculum vulgare*) is one of the most versatile garden plants in the family.

below *Oenanthe aquatica* next to water, a typical habitat for umbelliferous plants.

below right *Seseli gummiferum*, one of the umbellifers that gardeners should consider growing.

using umbellifers

A family of perennials and biennials bearing flat-topped umbels composed of many hundreds of tiny flowers, the umbellifers (or cow-parsley family) have, like grasses, been only recently exploited by gardeners. Many open and semi-shaded environments of northern Europe are dominated by such plants as cow-parsley (*Anthriscus sylvestris*) and wild parsnip (*Pastinaca sativa*) and it is probably this ubiquity, combined with the weedy tendencies of some wild species that has put gardeners off using them.

If you wish to evoke nature in the garden, however, there are few better families of plants to use. Their filigree flowers add such a touch of delicacy that those who use them wonder how they ever managed without them. Most are biennial or short-lived perennials which self-seed easily, making them suitable for a relaxed style of planting where the annual redistribution of a plant variety is all part of the effect. As the original parent plants die, their seedlings will appear the following spring. Most species flower in their first year, although some take two.

Plants such as *Chaerophyllum hirsutum* 'Roseum' or *Selinum wallichianum* are useful for lightly shaded places where most grasses may not thrive. Others, such as the purple-flowered *Angelica gigas* or *A. archangelica*, are more architectural, the latter growing flowerheads on stems 2m (6ft) high. These larger and more striking species tend to prefer sunny habitats. Some, however, such as fennel (*Foeniculum vulgare*), which forms a rounded, bush-like clump, flourish best in dry conditions.

Some umbellifers have much smaller, more tightly packed flowerheads than others. The astrantias, whose button-like heads are surrounded by a ruff of bracts, are invaluable in sunny or lightly shaded areas. The eryngiums too have tightly packed flowerheads, usually accompanied by spiny-looking leaves and bracts; they can be grown to good effect in the border or in gravel gardens with other plants from dry habitats.

Gardenworthy umbellifers with outstanding foliage

Anthriscus sylvestris 'Ravenswing'

Chaerophyllym hirsutum 'Roseum'

Meum athamanticum

Pimpinella major 'Rosea'

Selinum wallichianum and *S. tenuifolium*

Seseli gumniferum

Taller and more dramatic umbellifers

Angelica gigas

Angelica archangelica

Angelica atropurpurea

Ferula communis

Levisticum officinale

Molopospermum peloponnesiacum

Peucedanum verticillare

repetition & rhythm

When you admire a wild habitat like a wildflower meadow, it is not just the colours or shapes that are attractive, but the manner in which the flowers are scattered across a wide area in varying densities. Repetition generates a strong visual impact. Compare this with so many border treatments, where many varieties may only be represented by one individual, alongside clumps of some favoured varieties. There may be plenty of visual impact, but it is different. Often blotchy or broken up, there is a lack of visual continuity; when there are too many varieties in a border, there is nothing to hold the whole scene together.

Another reason why many modern mixed borders lack a sense of unity is simply that they comprise so many different elements: shrubs, perennial species, perennial hybrids, plants with variegated or coloured foliage, annuals, even vegetables. Where there is too much

variety, the eye cannot perceive a common theme, especially if there is a lot of vivid colours, and tinted or variegated foliage. In the borders proposed in this book, the plant selection is limited: only natural species or selections that are very similar to their wild ancestors. This in itself creates a strong sense of unity. Such plants are likely to share certain characteristics, and thus composing a planting exclusively with them will already have a certain theme, especially if the plant selection is made with some foresight, taking into consideration how plant communities work in nature: interspersing colourful perennials with grasses, for example.

above **The self-sowing of mulleins (*Verbascum* species) is always welcome for introducing an element of naturalistic rhythm into a planting.**

above right **Here pink is repeated by using *Eupatorium purpureum* 'Atropurpureum' and *Monarda* 'Purple Ann' and a mass grouping of *Lythrum virgatum*.**

right **Grasses, umbellifers and other umbel-shaped flowers are among the most useful for creating rhythm, familiar from their prominence in natural environments.**

Repeating certain species or shapes or colours is the obvious way to create rhythm. Repeating one particularly structural plant, such as an echinops, veronicastrum or *Eupatorium purpureum* 'Atropurpureum' gives a planting a strong rhythm. To develop a softer rhythm, use less strongly defined structural plants, such as thalictrum or filipendula. Another kind of rhythm is created by using a number of different plants which repeat a similar element from the planting palette: spires are the most potent form for achieving a good rhythm. Colour may be used too. If a particular shade is repeated several times in a border, a pattern will emerge.

A rhythm develops best over a number of years in a planting through the spontaneous process of self-sowing. Digitalis and verbascum are good examples. If there are too many seedlings, some should be weeded out or there is a danger that they will grow to overwhelm the rhythm.

assembling a planting

When you want to create a planting, you will have to select plants that you like and which you think will look good together. This is a much more subconscious process than people think; because we all have likes and dislikes, we tend to choose plants, or colours, or pictures, or furniture – or whatever – on a fairly consistent basis. Someone who likes yellow, for instance, will almost inevitably choose lots of yellow; that yellow will provide a sense of unity and therefore harmony.

Nevertheless, planting design has a lot to do with getting a feel for particular kinds of plant, reacting intuitively to the form, texture, colour and mood of plants. Then, once you have the feel for a particular garden mood, it will be easy to select plants, as you will often know instantly when you see a new plant whether it will fit in or not. It is this intuitive feel for what is right that is perhaps the most important part of creating a successful planting and why it is not possible for planting design to be learnt purely through a series of logical steps. An intimate familiarity with plants is essential. It is important that nothing is ever regarded as rigid. Gardening is a process, not an end result, and we should seize on the adaptability of perennials to be always ready to improve plantings by moving things around.

There is another side to designing a planting, however, which is to work out on paper what plant is to go where. Obviously, you will be using favourite plants, but actually drawing up a plan will draw your attention to certain key questions: which plants are to go next to each other; how many you will need to get; how they are to be distributed through the

left Pinks and purples dominate this planting, from *Scabiosa japonica* var. *alpina* to *Salvia verticillata*.

right This planting resembles a traditional perennial border, but uses different plants. At the front, clockwise, are *Achillea* 'Walther Funcke', *Phlox* 'Rosa Pastell', *Stipa gigantea*, *Persicaria amplexicaulis* 'Firedance', *Calamagrostis brachytricha*, *Helenium* 'Rubinzwerg', *Stipa calamagrostis* and *Achillea* 'Summerwine'. At the back are *Monarda* 'Squaw', *Eupatorium purpureum* 'Atropurpureum', *Helenium* 'Flammendes Käthchen', *Echinops ritro* 'Veitch's Blue', *Monarda* 'Comanche', *M.* 'Cherokee', *Agastache foeniculum* and *Persicaria amplexicaulis* 'Firetail'.

A good way to plan a border planting is to start with three tall structural plants at the back of the border, then work forward, relating each new layer of plants to the layer behind. The two groups can be used individually, or linked – letters indicate possibilities for linking plants.

GROUP 1

1 *Phlox paniculata* 'Lavendelwolke'

2 *Eupatorium purpureum* 'Atropurpureum'

3 *Filipendula rubra* 'Venusta'

4 *Sanguisorba officinalis*

5 *Monarda* 'Mohawk'

6 *Lythrum salicaria* 'Blush'

7 *Calamagrostis brachytricha*

8 *Achillea* 'Walther Funcke'

9 *Astrantia major* 'Claret'

10 *Saponaria* x *lempergii* 'Max Frei'

LINKING PLANTS

A *Molinia caerulea* 'Transparent'

B *Thalictrum lucidum*

C *Salvia verticillata* 'Purple Rain'

D *Scabiosa japonica* var. *alpina*

E *Digitalis ferruginea*

GROUP 2

1 *Veronicastrum virginicum* 'Fascination'

2 *Miscanthus sinensis* 'Malepartus'

3 *Aster novae-angliae* 'Violetta'

4 *Phlomis tuberosa* 'Amazone'

5 *Lobelia* 'Eulalia Berridge'

6 *Echinacea purpurea* 'Rubinstern'

7 *Phlox paniculata* 'Rosa Pastell'

8 *Eryngium bourgatii*

9 *Origanum* 'Rosenkuppel'

10 *Sedum* 'Munstead'

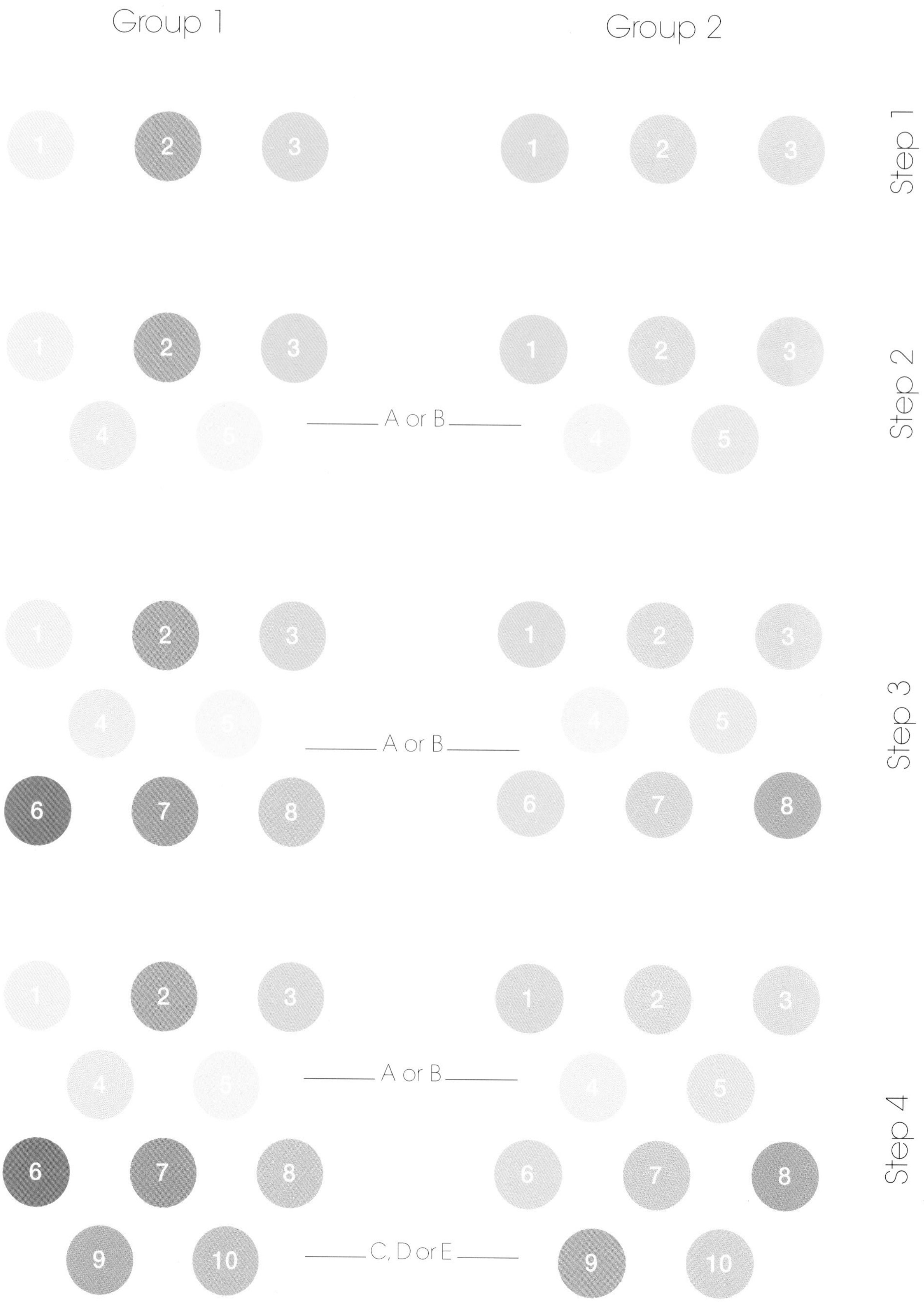

Group 1

Group 2

Step 1

Step 2

Step 3

Step 4

A or B

A or B

A or B

C, D or E

planting; and what you will do with the gaps, the places that you have not thought of, which will complement the ones you have designed already in your mind's eye.

Professional garden designers work with plans drawn to scale, where each plant is allocated a space on paper in proportion to the amount of ground it will cover. Some people find it relatively easy to interpret plans, to see the results in their imagination, but others find it impossible. One alternative to a plan is a diagram that shows a planting more or less as you would see it in real life – much easier to interpret. This can be drawn to scale too, showing the width of the plants in the border. And you could supplement this plan with a number of cross-sections which would show the border in depth.

When designing a planting, you should think first about the taller, structural plants with the longest season of interest, because they will be the backbone around which everything else is built. If you have enough space, it is good to use the same plant at intervals through the border, to create a sense of rhythm. Perhaps you are going to use three plants of *Eupatorium purpureum*

above *Calamagrostis* x *acutiflora* 'Karl Foerster' is fronted by monardas and *Phlox paniculata*. In the centre are *Lythrum salicaria* 'Zigeunerblut', *Dracocephalum rupestre* with *Artemisia absinthium* 'Lambrook Silver', *Sidalcea* 'My Love' and *Monarda* 'Balance' in the foreground. below Tall perennials like *Thalictrum polygamum* rise above more compact ones like *Phlox paniculata* 'Düsterlohe', *Campanula lactiflora* 'Loddon Anna', persicaria, *Verbena hastata* and *Filipendula rubra* 'Venusta'.

above left Colour acts as a unifying theme uniting a variety of different flower shapes. *Thalictrum lucidum* and the red-leaved annual *Atriplex hortensis* var. *rubra* provide scale and structure. In the front is orange-red *Helenium* 'Kupferzwerg', pale pink *Echinacea purpurea* seedling and dull red *Sedum telephium* 'Munstead Red'.

above right Spikes of dark purple *Lobelia* 'Tania' contrast with the wispy umbels of *Selinum wallichianum* and the large flowers of *Hemerocallis* 'Gentle Shepherd' (right). *Atriplex hortensis* var. *rubra* self-sows readily after its first year of cultivation making it a wild-card in the planning of the border. Without such spontaneous elements the border would definitely lack the hand of nature.

opposite *Strobilanthes atropurpurea*, *Panicum virgatum* 'Squaw' and *Persicaria amplexicaulis* 'Rosea' make an interesting combination.

'Atropurpureum' in a large border. Each one of these can be combined with one of another smaller species to create three pairs: one with a veronicastrum, one with a phlox and one with a filipendula, for example. These three combinations can then each be linked to some other plants, working downwards in size towards the front. You can add more large, structural plants to complement the original eupatorium and then repeat the process, until all the space is filled. Add filler plants last of all, with progressively more of them towards the front. And remember to match plant shapes within a group of plants from the planting palette, not just by comparing one variety to one other at random.

When the first draft of the planting plan is complete, you should look through it to check that there is a good distribution of different shapes and colours; dotting around clearly defined shapes like spires will give a sense of form and structure, which can be balanced by a liberal scattering of transparent plants, contributing air and lightness of touch. Check too that you have a good distribution of colours. It makes sense to have the tallest plants at the back and the shortest at the front in a border, simply so that everything can be seen; likewise, in a freestanding border where there is no backdrop, to have the taller plants in the middle. Sticking to this rule dogmatically, though, will result in a regimented appearance, recalling the highly disciplined borders of Edwardian England, where all the plants knew their place and there was no spontaneity.

There is more likely to be a feeling of movement within a planting if you position some taller plants near to the front of it. Narrow varieties that hide little create a more spontaneous look: *Digitalis ferruginea*, for example, which is likely to self-sow itself like this anyway. Grasses, or other plants which are effectively transparent, can be placed in the front or the middle of the border too; they will act as a thin veil behind which the other plants can be seen. Meanwhile, there is also scope for positioning bulkier, more solid plants at the front of the border, plants such as *Persicaria amplexicaulis* which partly obscure what is behind them, forcing the viewer to move around the planting and look at it from all angles to see what is concealed. It is, after all, an elementary rule of garden design that not everything in it should be visible on first glance. People will get more out of a garden if they are encouraged to explore it thoroughly and to discover certain things for themselves.

natural planting

above *Echinacea purpurea* 'Rubinstern' and the grass *Calamagrostis* x *acutiflora* 'Karl Foerster' make a strikingly natural combination which is reminiscent of many wildflower plantings.

opposite above Astrantias growing among wild grasses in an experimental planting. Naturalizing perennials in grass is only successful with carefully chosen species.

The notion that plants from particular habitats belong together in the garden carries some weight. Common sense dictates that species from a similar environment will thrive happily in garden situations roughly similar to those in which they flourish in nature. But, using this ecological basis to select plants can be limiting. The remarkable thing about gardens, at least in cool temperate climates, is how plants from disparate habitats can be accommodated cheek by jowl: perovskia from the dry steppe alongside moisture-loving persicarias, for example. The aim of this book is to show how to create an image of nature in the garden, not replicate it. So feel free to choose plants that might not have originated in similar habitats.

As a basic principle, if two plants grow well together in the garden, then that is good enough. However, it is important not to force them to try to grow together, as some traditional gardeners have tried to do, attempting to grow azaleas next to roses, for example. I do not believe in extensive soil modification in order to try to grow plants in soil in which they would not otherwise grow. Such practices inevitably involve environmental damage and are rarely successful in the long term.

A pragmatic approach to plant selection stresses a mixture of plants from a gradient of ecological suitability. Firstly, there are those species that are bound to do well in your garden, because they come from a very similar habitat. Then there are those from dissimilar habitats which your knowledge of gardening might suggest are adaptable to growing in a wide range of conditions. Finally there are those which can best be described as experiments; if they succeed, all well and good, but you must be prepared to adopt a phlegmatic attitude if they should fail. Climate plays an important role in how pragmatic our plant selection can be. Those gardening in more extreme climates or aspects – Mediterranean or maritime, for example – do have to be most aware of plant ecology. The broad selection of plants that can flourish together in a cool temperate climate, the context in which this book was written, may have to be examined more rigorously in order to identify suitable plants for a stressful environment.

below *Rudbeckia maxima* from the American prairies is happy growing next to *Macleaya cordata* from eastern Asia. Although they come from distant geographical areas, they thrive together in the garden as they are from similar climates.

Seasonal plantings in nature

The pattern of growth in wild habitats of different profiles can be considered when planning a planting scheme to look good all year.

Habitat:	Woodland area	Woodland edge	Meadow
Profile:	Partially shaded in spring and fully shaded in summer.	Light shade throughout the year.	Full sun throughout the year.
Plants:	Spring flowers: bulbs, ground-hugging perennials, shrubs.	Some spring bulbs and perennials.	Early bulbs and a very few small perennials.
	Some early summer, taller-flowering with good seedheads and skeletons.	Wide variety of flowering perennials, some shrubs.	A reasonable number of early summer perennials, and a few grasses.
	Some late-flowering with foliage interest through the season and and possible good winter interest.	Use the plants for interest after their flowering period too.	A wide range of large-growing, late-flowering perennials and grasses.

Traditional gardens, because of their focus on flowers, tend to look their best in spring and early summer; then, unless there is lots of summer bedding, go downhill. Gardening with perennials means that the main flowering season occupies most of the summer, with some species carrying on into autumn, and the dead stems and seedheads of perennials and grasses standing through winter.

It is possible to create mixed borders that provide interest practically all year round, with shrubs, climbers, perennials, bulbs and annuals organized so that there is always something worth looking at. But this means that the impact of the whole border is reduced because only a small part of it is at its best at any one time. Better perhaps to have a short piece whose final movement has all the orchestra playing, than an attenuated work which never really seizes the listener's attention.

Another drawback of the mixed, long season border is the length of time for which shrubs are appealing: they may look beautiful in the spring, but rarely do so later on.

left The luxuriance of late summer is demonstrated by *Eupatorium purpureum* 'Atropurpureum' and the pale pink discs of *Malva moschata* which have seeded into the planting spontaneously. Narrow paths such as this, that force you to plunge through a planting almost having to elbow stems out of the way, are a marvellous way of experiencing the lushness of this time of year.

right *Hosta* 'Moody Blues' has the freshness of new growth in late spring, alongside the pale red-pink flowers of *Tellima grandiflora*, the unfurling croziers of the fern *Polystichum setiferum* and the leaves of a cimicifuga and a hellebore. Most of the interest at this time of year is concentrated at a low level like this.

planting through the seasons

Few of them have outstanding shape or foliage and most take up far too much space. It is often possible to fit a dozen perennials into the space occupied by one shrub.

Looking at different plants that flower at different times of year it is clear that they fall into roughly three categories: spring-flowering woodlanders, early summer woodland edge species and later summer open meadow species. There are exceptions: the cowslips (*Primula veris*) which flower in spring meadows or the prairie crocus (*Pulsatilla patens*) that blooms early in the year, for example, or the late-flowering woodlanders like cimicifuga or *Eupatorium rugosum*. The basic point is that the majority of species of a type' of habitat look glorious for one season only.

A planting composed entirely of late-flowering perennials and grasses can be awe-inspiring, far more so than if they were forced to share space with large numbers of early-flowering species, let alone shrubs. You can always use smaller filler plants to provide colour earlier in the season, and include some bulbs among the larger plants, because their foliage will be dying before many of the perennials have even shown themselves above ground. Indeed, without any of this, the border risks being dull for the early part of the growing season.

In shade there are relatively few species that flower after early summer, and it would make sense to include some of these in any area given over to bulbs and spring-flowering perennials, otherwise there will be a long season with little but green. One or two spring-flowering shrubs will contribute the height and bulk that early perennials lack, and some shade-tolerant, early-flowering perennials can often be grown around the edge of the shrub canopy. Early summer-flowering species occupy a middle position, and to some extent they can be combined with either the spring-flowering woodlanders or the sun-loving late species.

selecting plants with good continuity

Plants with attractive foliage, stems or seedheads that continue to look good after flowering

Achillea filipendulina hybrids

Artemisia lactiflora (Guizhou group)

Aster umbellatus

Astilbe tacquetii cultivars

Cimicifuga

Digitalis, especially D. ferruginea

Eryngium, especially E. giganteum

Eupatorium species and cultivars

Filipendula (taller ones)

Gaura lindheimeri and G. 'Whirling Butterflies'

Gillenia

Iris ensata

Lavatera cachemiriana

Ligularia

Lysimachia ephemerum

Lythrum

Monarda

Phlomis tuberosa

Phlomis russeliana

Physostegia

Rodgersia

Rudbeckia

Salvia nemorosa or S. x sylvestris

Types of border sedum

Solidago

x Solidaster

Stachys monieri and S. officinalis

Thalictrum

Almost all umbellifers

Verbascum

Verbena

Veronicastrum

Vernonia and most grasses

Late-flowering perennials –

that have good foliage in the earlier part of the summer

Aster lateriflorus

Cimicifuga

Eupatorium purpureum 'Atropurpureum'

Grasses

Helianthus salicifolius

Kirengeshoma palmata

Tricyrtis formosana

Veronicastrum virginicum

that can be grown in shade among early-flowering species

Aconitum carmichaelii

Anemone hupehensis

Anemone japonica

Ceratostigma

Cimicifuga simplex Atropurpurea Group

Eupatorium purpureum 'Atropurpureum'

Kirengeshoma palmata

Sedum telephium and hybrids

x Solidaster luteus

Some plants flower for a short time, others for much longer: some are insignificant until they flower, others have attractive or elegant foliage; some die gracefully, others messily. Ensuring that you choose plants that have a long season of interest is important, especially if you are working with smaller plantings, where anything that is untidy or uninteresting is much more likely to be seen. Sometimes, though, plants with a short season can be put close together so that they cover for each other: *Papaver orientale*, which flowers in early summer and then dies back, can be put next to *Gypsophila paniculata*, which even as a relatively small plant produces a huge spray of flowers in midsummer, or *Persicaria amplexicaulis*, which flowers later still.

You should always include some plants that look good throughout the growing season in a planting, because they provide a sense of continuity and a sort of reliable backbone to a planting. Everything else may grow and wither around them but they stay looking tidy and good. *Eryngium giganteum* is such a choice, as it continues to look statuesque well into the winter after its early summer-flowering season. The clustered spires of the earlier-flowering cultivars of veronicastrum ('Temptation', 'Apollo' or 'Spring Dew', say) also retain their character for a long time.

A plant's winter appearance is an important aspect of its continuity. Plants that bear shapely seedheads and which are weather-resistant are particularly useful for a gardener seeking a long season (looked at in more detail on pages 140–143).

above right **A variety of plants that continue to look good after they have finished flowering.** *Filipendula rubra* **'Venusta' has pink plumes in midsummer which later die to rich brown heads.**

far right *Agastache foeniculum* **'Alabaster' has distinctive spires that here separate pale pink** *Monarda* **'Fishes' and dark orange** *Helenium* **'Kupferzwerg', all of which maintain the central parts of their flowerheads as persistent seedcases during the winter months.**

right *Cimicifuga simplex* **Atropurpurea Group stands tall above grasses in early autumn. It continues to feature until well into winter.**

Plants that sometimes flower twice, especially if dead flowers or older stems are removed

Many *Achillea*

Alchemilla mollis

Astrantia cultivars

Campanula lactiflora

Geranium endressii

G. x *oxonianum*

Types of *Nepeta* x *faassenii*
  and *N. racemosa*

Salvia nemorosa and
  S. x *superba* cultivars.

breaking the rules

Many people are put off gardening by what they see as the 'rules' – the dogma of centuries about things that you should and should not do in the garden. Every gardener needs to develop his or her own vision, and this entails experimenting, taking risks, trying out new plants, techniques and schemes, seeing which ones work and which do not.

To be a successful gardener you need to understand the basics of how plants grow, and how they develop over time. This will give you a perspective on plants that is more fundamental than is often stated in books, but which will enable you to begin to question the rules in an intelligent way. For example, books often state that perennials should be cut down in the autumn, without any explanation as to why. Any experience we have gained about plants in the wild would suggest that this rule looks absurd – for while perennials may be mown during the growing season along roads, or munched by grazing animals, there is nothing in nature to cut down wild perennials in the autumn, every autumn. The rule, then, seems to have nothing to do with success or failure in cultivation; instead, it is more to do with human intolerance of nature's untidiness.

To summarize, if a rule has an explanation that has to do with successful cultivation, there is probably a good reason for it. If it does not, then it may well be a dogma, with little foundation. Much of what is written about designing plantings falls into the latter category: advice about not putting two plants together of the same colour; putting the tallest plants at the back and the shortest at the front, for example. Many of these rules are founded in an aesthetic that plays with very safe harmonies. Being adventurous is, to a large extent, about playing around with contrast. How much contrast you enjoy is a very personal matter. If you find lots of strong colours and powerful plant shapes appealing, so be it. It is your garden, and it is entirely up to you to make the rules about what it looks like.

far left Climbers are ultimately flexible plants, and are wide open to a variety of innovative uses. This is *Hydrangea anomala* subsp. *petiolaris*, a shrubby climber that is here trained onto an arched frame so that it grows into a tree-like shape. The perennial at the bottom left developing autumn tints is the ivy relative *Aralia racemosa*, noted for its bold foliage.

above left The dead leaves of *Eupatorium purpureum* 'Atropurpureum' are a dark counterpoint to brighter autumn tints.

left *Monarda* seedheads among wispy *Molinia* with a backdrop of *Sanguisorba canadensis* spires.

evolution

The traditional herbaceous border involved a great deal of work. Such borders needed intensive feeding with large quantities of manure every autumn. Many of the plants needed to be divided every year or every few years if they were to remain healthy. Many of the tall but heavy-flowering stems also needed staking as they were prone to collapse. Unfortunately, all this has prejudiced many people against perennial borders; it is perhaps not surprising that the lower-maintenance 'mixed border' has become a more popular form.

The perennial plantings examined in this book are quite different to these traditional, high-maintenance borders. To start with, the selection of plants is different, and the new emphasis on natural species or selections from natural species means that the flowers are more in proportion with the plants, making the border less top-heavy and reducing the need for staking. Natural species often need less intensive feeding too. Indeed, most perennials do not need large quantities of nutrients; they may grow much more lush, but they will probably grow uncharacteristically top-heavy, and will often flop over.

Generally, you should choose long-lived plants for a perennial border and those that do not need frequent division. Include self-seeding short-lived species, which constantly renew themselves, such as species of digitalis, verbascum and *Eryngium giganteum*.

Although most perennials do not need a great deal of feeding, you may have to improve particularly poor soils – very sandy or stony soil, for example – by adding quantities of humus-producing material such as manure, compost or slow-release organic fertilizers. Alternatively, you could limit yourself, when you select your plants, to species that are known to be tolerant of poor soils.

establishment and maintenance

Perennials establish themselves very quickly, especially compared to woody plants; many perennial plantings are effectively mature after only three years. However, many taller perennials may not develop a very strong root system during the first year after planting which means that they might need support, and the young plants may also need some form of irrigation during this first year.

Moreover, the perennial border does still require some maintenance: there are two essential tasks. Firstly, all the dead growth needs to be cleared away during the dormant season. Traditionally, dead growth would be cut back in autumn. As the pictures on pages 140–143 show, however, dead stems can have a beauty of their own, and gardeners would do better to choose either not to cut back too early, or to cut back selectively, removing only stems that have become unattractive or messy. Dead material should either be composted, to be returned to the border in the future, or shredded and used as a mulch. Leaving dead stems has practical advantages too: they provide some frost protection for buds at ground level; the seedheads and the insect life they support will be an important source of food for birds; and, if you wish to re-plant any of the border during the winter, dead stems give you a much better idea of what is where than cut stems.

The other essential maintenance task is weeding, for the aggressive plant species that compete with perennials need to be kept in check. If the site for the planting has been freed of perennial weed roots, the problem will be limited to dealing with those that blow in, or sprout from 'the seed bank'; those buried in the top layer of soil.

Where it is obvious that the seed bank is large, where countless seedlings pop up every time the soil is disturbed, a mulch will help to eliminate the germination of the vast majority of these seeds. A wood-chip or bark mulch is the most effective, but this can only be applied once the entire perennial planting is in place. Moreover, it is vital that only material that has been composted for at least a year is used, as fresh mulch may contain toxins.

In borders with no mulch, some weed seed will inevitably germinate. This is less of a problem between early summer and autumn because the thick growth of perennials will cover the soil and prevent most weed growth. But, in maritime climates with a long growing season, there is a period between late winter and late spring, and sometimes in early winter too, when weed growth is considerable, necessitating their removal. Particular attention should be paid to weeds that begin to establish themselves in the crowns of perennials, as this is a singularly difficult place from which to remove them.

far left There is little room for weeds to grow among burgeoning late summer perennial growth like this. During the earlier part of the year though there is much more bare earth that acts as an attractive seedbed for them.

left *Molinia caerulea* with a miscanthus in the background. Such glowing colours lit by the low autumn and winter sunlight are denied to gardeners who follow the unnecessary and destructive practice of tidying up in the autumn.

below Very wide borders can be transected by narrow paths which facilitate maintenance. To the bottom left of the planting is *Saponaria* x *lempergii* 'Max Frei'.

using plants as architecture

So far everything in this book has pointed towards the importance of learning from nature. Gardening, however, is about creating a balance between nature and art, and distinctive garden styles can be created along the gradient between art (formality) and nature (wildness). I super-impose two layers in my gardens: the formality of an underlying framework or of particular pieces, and then the perennials and grasses. The static formal layer comprises hedges, clipped forms, paths and the outlines of borders, and is a fixed reference point against which the intense changes experienced in the seasonally dynamic perennial planting layer are a constantly changing contrast.

hedges

Hedges are essential as background, and to create privacy, either to enclose the whole garden or to make 'rooms' within it. If there are hedges in the landscape, the garden hedges will mirror them, involving landscape and garden with each other. If you are creative, it is possible to cut hedges in all sorts of dynamic ways: in curves to look like a dragon's back, or in a more geometrical zig-zag. You can also plant hedges creatively, using a mixture of evergreens, like yew, alongside deciduous species, such as field maple (*Acer campestre*), larch (*Larix* species), hornbeam (*Carpinus betulus*), species of amelanchier, dogwood (*Cornus mas*) and beech (*Fagus sylvatica*). Allowed to grow naturally, the branches will blend into each other, creating a marbled effect, but it is also possible to create a very dramatic effect if you keep the plants separate using steel plates. Moreover, people often think that only an evergreen hedge has anything to offer in winter, but the interlocking branches of the skeletons in a mixed deciduous hedge can be just as attractive, each individual species having a different pattern of branching.

perspectives within the garden

A garden will provide pleasure every day if, from the house, it offers an exciting view of a border, a pond, a clipped shrub, a statue, or an axis ending in a group of trees. Within the garden a perspective is like a spinal cord for the whole garden, especially if there is a path that runs along the course of this axis.

The kind of perspective that characterized classically formal gardens was, to my mind at least, too formulaic, however; everything was generally articulated at right angles off a central axis – too predictable an arrangement, which could be regarded as a weakness in the overall design. It can also mean that the viewer looks straight down a vista to a statue or similar eye-catcher at the end and that is it; the effect is shallow. If you take this classical axis and twist it a little, however, it is transformed. Dig an elliptical border instead of a circular one in the middle of your axis;

opposite All power to the imagination should be the slogan when dealing with clipping and training plants to make architectural features. There is no reason why the dogmatic rules of classical formality should have a stranglehold over the art of plant shaping. A window cut into a hedge here allows an enticing view through to a garden.

left Deciduous hedging cut into organic flowing shapes is most effective in the winter, when the patterns made by the branching are a feature in their own right.

below A yew clipped into a simple abstract shape is a distinctly modernist version of a very traditional art form. Such features make a welcome and restful change of pace in gardens bursting with flowers and colour .

or, if you intend to line your axis with an avenue of clipped yews, give them a twist too, so that they are staggered, so that you create a different kind of symmetry, a zig-zag symmetry, which forces the eye to move from side to side, thus viewing the garden much more thoroughly than it would if it were drawn directly to the vanishing point of the perspective.

paths and lawns

It is important to introduce as many adventures into the garden as possible, and paths will provide you with a means to encourage the viewer to explore particular places, or to participate in illusions. A small path leading into a shrubbery at the back of a garden, for example, will create the illusion that there is still something else to explore.

Traditionally, a border would be planted to be viewed from the front, from a path or lawn, but imagine how much more exciting it would be to savour a border's beauty from several different angles; having a narrow

path that skirts around the edge of a border through an area of lower-growing plants, for example, and one that goes around behind the border, giving the viewer the opportunity to see the plants from several different angles. Such paths bring the visitor face to face with the plants in the border in a very intimate way, encouraging them to look at the plants in a completely new way. Indeed, walking down a path like this through tall, late-summer perennials is like taking a walk through a wild prairie.

Lawns are essential in medium-sized or larger gardens as empty green spaces. One may be needed for practical reasons (if you have children who need space to play games, or if you want to sunbathe or throw big parties) or merely as a restful green void, free from the excitement and stimulation thrust upon us by plants. If you do not cut the further reaches too regularly, a lawn can give a good sense of depth to your garden. With some imaginative mowing you can also etch pathways and patterns into them, adding another creative dimension.

finding places for borders

You will need plenty of space for a border or planting created for summer and autumn perennials, unsurprisingly when you consider that it is the high point of the perennial year, and that many of the plants are substantial. Such a planting may well include quite a bit of backdrop, a wall or hedge, as borders have traditionally done, but the plants should have enough space so they do not hug this backdrop; instead they should appear to flow outwards from it, perhaps with paths running through the border itself.

Borders for spring-flowering plants can be much more intimate in scale, and are most easily enjoyed if sited quite near the house. The bulbs and woodland-floor plants of spring look most at home when they are grown alongside spring-flowering shrubs and trees, and thrive in light, even full shade under trees, although they will struggle if the soil is full of roots and dry. North- and east-facing aspects which offer either shade or relatively cool conditions are also suitable. To maintain the interest in spring borders through summer, though, it may be necessary to make use of species such as pulmonarias and ferns, which have attractive leaves, or the odd late-flowering perennial.

far left A bracelet of brick and yew encloses an island planted with *Carex muskingumensis* and the grass *Miscanthus sinensis* 'Malepartus' making a very simple and effective garden feature which is attractive all year round.

above A seat by Paul Anderson at the end of a path over which *Centranthus ruber, Monarda* 'Fishes' and salvia cultivars spill. Such planting softens the edges of hard surfaces.

left The jointing pattern of this paving encourages the eye to sweep from side to side, slowing down the pace at which the borders are appreciated.

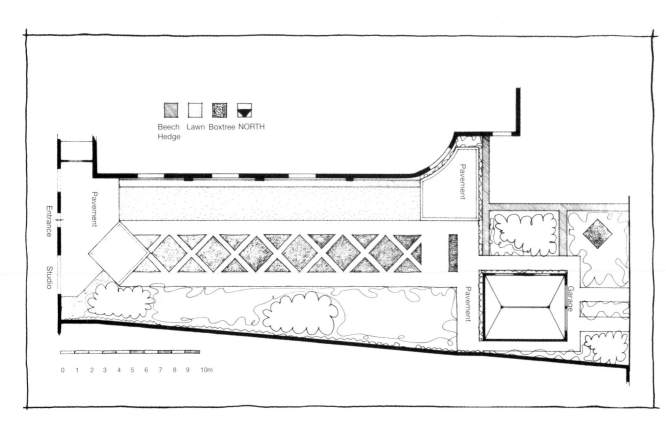

Beech Hedge Lawn Boxtree NORTH

0 1 2 3 4 5 6 7 8 9 10m

below left Using the lines of classical formality, but an innovative use of box and yew, this formal garden is separated by a hedge from the rest of the garden which is full of broad sweeps of perennial planting.
below and plan left A radical juxtaposition of box hedging and a narrow perennial border in a town garden.
right In the sales area at the Oudolf nursery in Hummelo, silver pears (*Pyrus salicifolia*) are clipped into rectangular columns, providing interest but without shading the plants or obstructing customers and staff.

clipped forms and pillars

Clipped pillars or blocks, of yew or other twiggy plants, can be used to interrupt the flow of a planting, punctuating a border, and encouraging people to stop and look and question. It is possible to use steel frames both to train the plants and to provide a visual framework until the plants have grown. Be adventurous when you select the plants you are going to train as pillars: *Pyrus salicifolia* can be used for its silver foliage, or *Cornus mas* or species of chaenomeles, which flower in early spring. Climbers such as clematis, the orange-berried *Celastrus orbiculatus*, or wisteria can also be easily trained to grow on steel frames of suitable heights.

These living pillars should not be used as one-off features, but as part of a series; regularly spaced, they provide rhythm and repetition right through the year. In this way it is possible to generate a sense of human order amid the sculptural forms of wild nature.

On a smaller scale, clipped blocks of arborescent ivy (*Hedera helix* 'Congesta' or *H. h.* 'Erecta') are rather modest and stand out most effectively amongst lower-growing ground cover. Certain characteristically upright plants, such as *Calamagrostis* x *acutiflora* 'Karl Foerster', can have a notably pillar-like effect, as can some grasses – *Molinia* 'Windspiel' and 'Karl Foerster', for example.

formal areas

Features such as clipped pillars and hedges can be used to provide an element of formality within the garden. This is a relatively traditional way of creating the aesthetic tension between formality and informality that lies at the heart of so many successful gardens, and we have already seen how it can be given an imaginative and contemporary twist.

It is also possible to generate this creative tension by physically separating formal areas from the rest of the garden, either by a hedge – whether a high hedge that actually blocks the view, or a lower one that creates more of a psychological barrier – or simply by the creation of a formal planting that occupies a defined and substantial territory of its own. For example, you could intersperse paths with regular clumps of clipped box, or create a series of alternating box and gravel squares, separated from the rest of the garden by a dramatic diagonal: box formality on one side, burgeoning perennial planting on the other. Having large islands of trimmed box or yew, or frameworks supporting clipped *Cornus mas* or other shrubs are other possibilities. The formality here acts as a block, an alternative to the rich tapestry of the perennial border, a restful space just as a lawn might be. The issue here is the creation of areas of simplicity, as against complexity.

With the effect of the simplicity of these one or two clipped shrubs in your mind's eye, think laterally about the creative use of mass planting and monoculture. In large spaces it is possible to use broad masses of a particular plant, such as a *Salvia nemorosa* hybrid, to create rivers and lakes of colour among banks of other plants.

ponds

Formal, geometrically regular ponds are appropriate near the house, while more organic shapes look better further away. The formal pond is more important as a shape, as a design element in itself, and requires only a few aquatic plants, while the latter can be made an integral part of a whole ensemble of moisture-loving plants, almost like a border built around water, with marginal plants obscuring the edges,' and big-leaved perennials like *Darmera peltata*, and reedy grasses like miscanthus, being reflected in the water. Many, if not most, of the large dramatic perennials that look their best late in the season, are, in fact, moisture-loving plants. To plant such species around a natural-looking body of water and to see their reflections not only enhances their own grandeur but also creates a highly evocative scene which almost inevitably dominates the area of the garden in which it is situated.

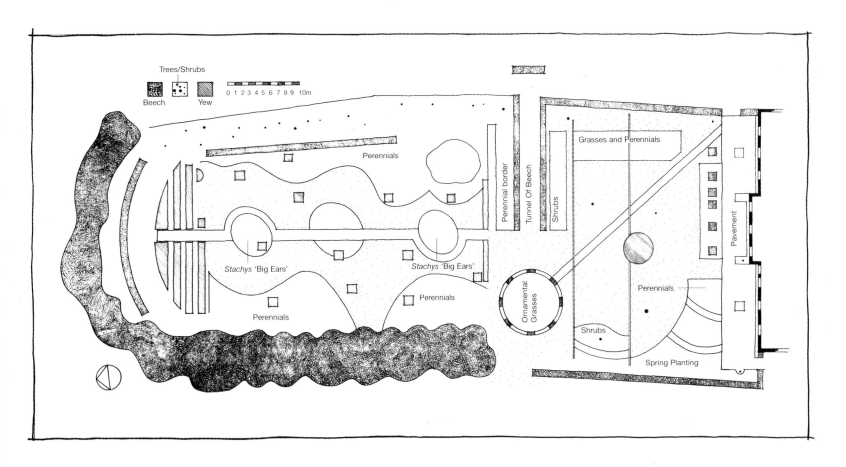

Trees/Shrubs

Beech   Yew

0 1 2 3 4 5 6 7 8 9 10m

Perennials

Stachys 'Big Ears'   *Stachys* 'Big Ears'

Perennials

Perennials   Perennials

Perennial border

Tunnel Of Beech

Shrubs

Grasses and Perennials

Pavement

Ornamental Grasses

Perennials

Shrubs

Spring Planting

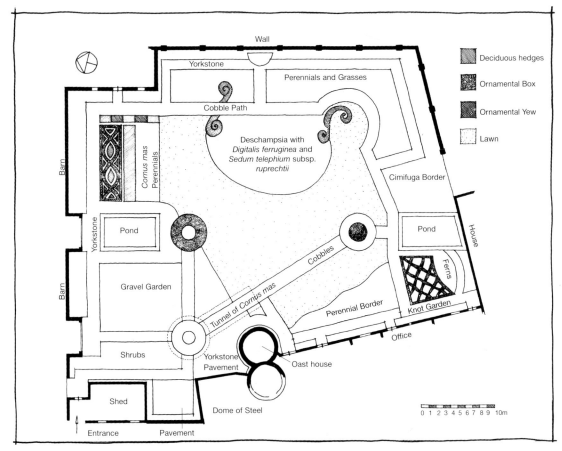

Wall

Yorkstone

Cobble Path

Perennials and Grasses

Deschampsia with *Digitalis ferruginea* and *Sedum telephium* subsp. *ruprechtii*

Cimifuga Border

Pond   Pond

Cornus mas Perennials

Yorkstone

Barn

Barn

Pond

Gravel Garden

Tunnel of *Cornus mas*

Cobbles

Perennial Border

Ferns

Knot Garden

House

Office

Shrubs

Yorkstone Pavement   Oast house

Shed

Dome of Steel

Entrance   Pavement

Deciduous hedges

Ornamental Box

Ornamental Yew

Lawn

0 1 2 3 4 5 6 7 8 9 10m

opposite **A theatrical layering of yew at the rear of the Oudolf garden, shown at the far left of the plan above.**

above **Notice how the axis changes from the diagonal in the part of the garden nearest the house as far as the bracelet shown on page 84, and then becomes spinal for the main part of the garden, with a series of off-centre beds, and staggered yew columns and wide perennial borders at each side. On the bottom left corner of the plan is the dragonback hedge shown on page 91.**

left **The garden at Bury Court, Hampshire, England. It is enclosed by walls and traditional farm buildings. The central area is lawn, with borders of large perennials chiefly to one side shown on pages 66 and 85, and a meadow of *Deschampsia*, a gravel garden, two ponds or tanks and a number of clipped shrub features.**

combining perennials with woody plants

Trees and shrubs can play an important role in gardens: as background, as a source of colour in spring, and to provide a sense of scale. Perennials often benefit from having a background of trees, shrubs or a hedge; their bulk helps to shelter perennials from potentially damaging winds. Visually, though, perennials do not need a backdrop of shrubs, as they have more than enough personality to stand alone, especially when combined with grasses.

Nor, in a practical sense, are shrubs and perennials ideal companions. In the early stages of planting, perennials have the upper hand, as they grow so much faster and can make it difficult for young shrubs or trees to get established. Later on, however, the competitive root systems which many shrubs develop will limit the growth of nearby perennials. Indeed, the roots of trees can be as much a problem for perennials as their shade. It is the small trees – species of prunus or malus and the spring- and early summer-flowering shrubs, such as viburnums, ligustrum and philadelphus, that have the most competitive root systems: midsummer-flowering shrubs such as buddleja or tamarix are less of a problem. In addition, some of these kinds of shrubs can be cut back to the ground or to a short stump every two years, which limits their size, especially valuable in restraining buddleja. Spring-flowering shrubs have no place in the summer border, as they take up so much space and offer practically nothing in return. It is better to use clipped shrubs, whose architectural qualities contribute so much more.

Perennials that can tolerate the root competition of shrubs

Alchemilla	Hosta
Brachypodium sylvaticum	Lamium
Carex	Luzula
Deschampsia	Melica
Digitalis	Milium effusum
Geranium, especially G. phaeum	Phlox (creeping varieties)
Hakonechloa	Pulmonaria
Helleborus	Omphalodes
Heuchera	Vinca

Shrubs that complement perennials without problems of competition

Amorpha	Cytisus
Buddleja	Hydrangea
Bupleurum	Indigofera
Caryopteris	Lespedeza
Ceanothus x pallidus 'Marie Simon' and other late summer-flowering ceanothus	Leycesteria
	Rhus
Cistus	Sambucus
Cllerodendron bungei	Tamarix
Cornus	Vitex
Cotinus coggygria	

views beyond the garden

Most people will want to incorporate an attractive surrounding landscape into their garden design somehow, as the age-old tradition of 'borrowed landscape' testifies. A surround of hedges and shrubs will only act like a old city wall if it has no openings through which to see the landscape beyond. Those in rural areas will often particularly want to link garden and landscape, or at least see their surroundings.

There is a major difference between flat and hilly landscapes in the way that scenery can be involved in the garden. In hilly regions, a view is often there whether we want it or not, and is often two-dimensional, like a screen. The skilful gardener may be able to selectively block out parts of it through judicious planting. In flat landscapes, it is harder work to involve a landscape in a garden but a completely different experience; you look through your surroundings to the distance, creating a more three-dimensional effect with a sense of perspective usually lacking elsewhere.

In a country garden you will find it easier to relate your garden to its surroundings if you incorporate elements that reflect those in the landscape; such links will extend the garden outwards, making it feel bigger. You can plant trees and shrubs in the garden that are locally native, for example, and in near water you could use miscanthus grasses to remind the viewer of reeds.

above Climbers trained onto mushroom-shaped frames form a partial barrier at the back of the stock beds at the Oudolf nursery in Hummelo. The beds here contain a collection of plants that are used for trialling and propagation.

left A dragonback hedge, originally a traditional hedge marking a boundary, with a variety of undulating curves. Neighbouring farmers have now started to copy it.

moods

introduction

Some gardens, particularly those created by landscape architects, are like monuments: frozen. Gardening, however, is a living process, which is why this book proposes the creation of something that changes through the years, even from day to day – the opposite, in fact, of a frozen garden. A garden that shows the cyclical nature of the gardening process is one that has emotion and mood.

Emotion and mood are vital to the success of a garden but receive remarkably little attention in books about design. They are qualities, however, that are very difficult to define in hard-and-fast terms; it is always difficult to describe why certain gardens are attractive and not others. It is even more difficult to write prescriptions for creating different moods, for mood is something that can only be planned into a garden to a limited extent. So many other factors are involved: much depends upon surroundings and the weather, on wind and light, over which we have only limited control. But if you accept certain conditions as givens, you can work with them and create garden moods that make the most of their circumstances.

Town gardens, for example, can be very claustrophobic, with high walls, and surrounding buildings that seem to tower over the garden. Yet those qualities can be exploited to give the garden a feeling of seclusion and intimacy. The walls may be clothed with climbers, for example, and large grasses or bamboos may be used to emphasize the power of nature. In this way we can reclaim the space for ourselves and for our vision of nature.

A garden in a very windswept and exposed place, where there may be little protection from the elements, poses the opposite problem. In time it may be possible to grow high hedges and trees to form some sort of windbreak, but do you really want to shut yourself off from your surroundings? Open country often has the most fantastic skies, where you look up and see a whole hemisphere of moving clouds above you; to shut out that sky would be a shame. Think about the plants that look good blowing in the wind: big reed-like grasses; smaller grasses; tall, strong-stemmed perennials; shrubs with whippy branches. Every garden has some aspect that can

be incorporated into a mood. It may be the light at one time of day or the overall quality of light – or the opposite: a particular quality of shade. It may be a view, of surrounding country, buildings or trees, that can be incorporated in the garden. Making the most of the 'genius of the place', as eighteenth-century designers termed it, is a process that involves getting to know your garden intimately over a long period of time, and being open to influences that may be very subtle and not easily articulated.

Gardens situated in different cultures have different moods. A garden can evoke feelings that relate to certain places and experiences, usually at a subconscious and emotional level. By working with an appropriate physical environment, using plants, hard landscaping and features that have particular associations for our memories, it is often possible to generate a particular mood of time and place. An open, sunny garden might be the ideal place for a Mediterranean garden, for example: using grey-leaved, evergreen shrubby species, stipa grasses, thistle-like perennials, verbascums and dwarf bulbs, combined with some formal elements, such as lines of clipped shrubs or herbal plants like lavender and rue, you could evoke the typical features of Mediterranean gardens.

Obviously, the plants you choose to use will be a key factor in whether you manage to create a particular mood in your garden. Some plants, because they have bold foliage cut into striking patterns, or are very tall, or have leaves of a size that dominate their surroundings, will evoke a sense of drama and dynamism: acanthus, echinops, eryngium, rodgersia, rheum or the big grass *Miscanthus floridulus*, for example. Others generate a soft, misty romanticism, stirring up memories of traditional hay meadows or old cottage gardens; these are generally species with lots of small blooms, especially those in which the flowers are gathered in large sprays, although arching stems, fine leaves, grasses with masses of hazy flower- or seedheads also help to create this nostalgic mood. Wild species of aster, like *Sanguisorba*, or cultivars like 'Tanna', that manage to retain the grace of their wild relatives would be ideal, as would the sprays of gypsophila species, umbellifers like peucedanum, myrrhis and selinum and many grasses too.

Finally, mood in gardens also involves time, for although all too often a garden's beauty only seems to live up to preconceived notions of what a beautiful garden should be in certain 'desirable' conditions, a garden in fact lives through all the different times of day, seasons of the year and experiences all the prevailing weather. Learning to appreciate gardens is thus also about discovering their assets whatever they look like at a particular time, seeing their beauty in mist, fog, rain, frost and snow, summer and winter, sunrise and sunset. You need to learn to appreciate the naked beauty of plant skeletons, for plants in a state of decay are also beautiful.

above A huge variety of plants contribute to garden mood, particularly those which alter as they grow, or which move. Grasses and other plants close to their wild ancestors have a delicacy which makes them responsive to the weather, and are a vital part of creating a sense of emotion.

light

Light is crucial and yet most garden designers devote little attention to the way it falls on plants; it is as if they know only one kind of light: flat and frontal. Yet there are many different kinds of light: the low, warm light of early morning or evening; the sideways light of winter, which can backlight the most humble grass of a lawn beautifully; and the hard light of clear summer days that etches shadows sharp against the ground.

The different kinds of light can transform the way that plants look, so it makes sense to position those plants to receive the maximum benefit. The same plant can look different depending on whether it is lit from behind or in front. The individual flowers of *Stipa gigantea*, for example, shimmer in the light, especially when seen against a darker background, while nearer to the ground, salvias – with their rows of calyces after the flowers have fallen – seem to come alive when lit from behind. A plant can also have a number of different faces if it is illuminated at only specific times of day. Yet these dramatic transformations are often denied the attention of the spectator simply because the plant is poorly positioned.

The flower- and seedheads of grasses catch light easily, and look especially beautiful when they are wet and covered in hundreds of beads of moisture. So you can

The globular flowerheads of *Echinops* are hard and clearly defined shapes, yet when they are backlit by late-afternoon sun they take on another, more ethereal dimension.

grasses to catch the light

Stipa calamagrostis
  Elongated heads of fine mauve flowers catch light in mid- to late summer.

Molinia
  Starburst sprays of fine, thrusting, brown stems are warmly illuminated by low autumn sunshine.

Panicum virgatum
  A mist of flowerheads held high over the dying leaves in autumn catch specks of sun like motes of dust.

Stipa gigantea
  An explosion of long stems carrying panicles of widely spaced oat-like heads, each one lit by the orangey tones of morning or evening sun.

Miscanthus sinensis varieties
  Grasses – medium to tall – with creamy, silver, pink or brown flowers in autumn, and seedheads in winter.

either plant rows of grasses like molinia and calamagrostis, to catch light in this way, or scatter them through a planting to provide highlights. Clumps of miscanthus will glow silver in the winter. Monardas and asters are light-catchers too, each individual flower transmitting the light slightly differently, depending on whether the light is coming from in front or from behind.

Light is very transitory. In summer, it can be very harsh and unflattering during the middle of the day, so early-morning and evening light tend to produce better effects. It is easier to appreciate the quality of colours in these moderate lights too, although the two ends of the spectrum behave in very different ways: blues are very effective under a low light, while reds become darker and darker until they eventually disappear.

Autumn and winter lights are low, illuminating plants from the side. They are also weak and around for only a relatively short period each day. So careful siting of plants that are going to benefit from their transformatory power is important to make the most of the light that exists. Plant growth is often thinner, however, so this low light has more opportunity to create subtle effects, creeping in among the plants and playing on parts that summer light does not, simply because there is less growth to get in the way.

above left **Salvia verticillata** 'Purple Rain' has bracts that appear dusky purple when lit from the front but which, when backlit, glow more softly, giving a subtler and more hazy effect. Thinking carefully about where to position a plant can make all the difference.

above middle Bamboo leaves, especially those with smaller leaves (like this *Phyllostachys aureosulcata*) can be used to capture light, and, because they move in the slightest breeze, they are particularly effective when lit against a darker background.

Plant and foliage colours in autumn and winter are very muted, for there are few flowers and many perennials are variations on a spectrum that ranges from straw yellow to dark brown. Yet many dead stems that appear dull and bled of colour and life under a grey sky can be transformed as soon as the sun shines, each subtle variation in this limited spectrum coming to life, the yellows positively glowing, the browns radiating a rich russet and the very darkest colours forming contrasting points of shadow. Positioned carefully, seedheads can be particularly spectacular when backlit – those with fluffy seeds such as ligularias, for example.

Spring light is clearer than autumn light, and given the fact that early-season growth tends to be ground-hugging, there is less scope for magical effects. To be lit by shafts of sunlight, plants need to be very carefully positioned; but colours can be given intensity by being backlit by low, spring light, while the young leaves of wood rushes (*Luzula* species) and unfolding fern fronds glow green in the early morning. Generally, though, young spring growth stands out well against the contrasting dark earth, whatever the light conditions. Plants with bronze- or red-tinted young growth are a particular feature of spring, and these often form attractive combinations with blue flowers.

above right **Low autumn sunlight contains just the right sort of warm tones to pick out the subtleties of dying perennials. Here the dark buttons of *Echinacea purpurea* and the straw-yellow stems of *Miscanthus* 'Flamingo' are lit to perfection.**

next page **Light on *Deschampsia cespitosa* 'Goldtau' illuminates millions of tiny seedheads – contrasting the effects created by the larger *Stipa offneri* and *S. turkestanica* (right). The architectural central plant is *Eryngium pandanifolium*, with *Verbena bonariensis* at the front.**

Plants that can snatch the light from the air need space, not to be hemmed in by walls, hedges or other plants. This is why grasses and plants with a transparent quality often look better in a more 'open' border. Planting to catch the light cannot really be planned on paper alone, for light is unpredictable, so when you are walking around the garden look out for special light effects, notice where they occur, and try to work out why they occur. It may then be possible to plant or replant to make the most of these effects. Bear in mind that the addition of a few more grasses somewhere where backlighting creates a dramatic effect, for instance, may be more valuable than a clump in another part of the garden where this effect cannot be reproduced.

Light, as artists have long been telling us, is very different in different regions of the world: areas with a Mediterranean climate have a very clear light, which can be quite brutal for much of the day during the summer, while the soft grey light of wetter and more changeable climates is better for subtle lighting effects. Light at the coast can be particularly strong, but not usually harsh, which is potentially rewarding.

left The low evening sunlight backlights a grass giving an impression of tranquillity – *Deschampsia cespitosa* 'Goldschleier' – along with the button heads of *Eryngium giganteum*. The red flower to the left of the planting is a helenium.

above The flowers on the spires of *Digitalis ferruginea* and *Agastache foeniculum* lit up in the early morning while their cores are left dark. Visible to the bottom right-hand corner are *Perovskia atriplicifolia* and *Persicaria amplexicaulis*.

movement

It is difficult to think of a garden where everything stands still: a classical formal garden, perhaps, where there is no natural spontaneity, and nothing of a sufficiently fine texture to move in a breeze. In gardens full of perennials and grasses, it does not take long to find something that is moving, even on the most windless summer's day.

Movement is one of the characteristics of life, so we associate it with energy and dynamism; a garden of movement responds to nature and feels alive, whereas one that is still seems almost dead.

Of all garden plants, perennials and grasses are the ones that register movement best: whether in response to a breath of wind, a sparrow launching itself into the air, or a human visitor handling a flower, they move easily and reverberate for a long time afterwards. Those with long stems and heavier flower- or seedheads are particularly sensitive registers of movement: the wand-like stems of the perennial dieramas, for example. Practically all grasses have such delicate flower- or seedheads that they move with the slightest breeze. Some have individual parts that move in their own individual rhythm, such as *Stipa gigantea* with its big panicles, while most, such as

Being entirely wind-pollinated, grasses depend upon air movement for their pollination, so it is entirely appropriate that they register its motion more expressively than do other plants.

plants to provide movement

Dierama pulcherrimum
pendent flowers on arching wand-like stems.

Epilobium angustifolium var. *album*
Seedheads of white fluff stand in clumps and move in unison.

Miscanthus sacchariflorus
A reed-like grass which is responsive to the wind because of its height.

Molinia caerulea 'Windspiel'
Fine heads on tall, almost straight stems, catching even the slightest breeze.

Sanguisorba officinalis
The small, blood-red bobbles borne on branching stems by the large Asiatic forms of this species are in almost constant motion.

Stipa gigantea
A grass which sways in the wind, with large, open panicles of dangling heads.

Stipa pulcherrima
The short-lived, long, feathery awned flowers of this grass seem to float on the air and are simply never still.

Calamagrostis brachytricha or *Stipa calamagrostis*, have heads that move in unison, creating a more large-scale effect. Those with unidirectional heads, like the miscanthus, tend to bow with their heads all curving through the same arc; all, of course, leaning away from the wind at the same time. This is why these grasses are so valuable if you want to imitate the movement of reedbeds in the wind. If you scatter lots of the same species of grass around the garden, you will be able to capture the magical pattern of waves that wind creates in fields of cereals or long grass, or that chance gust of wind catching and tossing some clumps into movement before others. Imagine, for a moment, the progress of the gust across the garden, the grasses moving with a rhythm as they bow and then spring back up.

Movement of course gives rise to sound, which has long been a very underrated element in traditional garden design. Logically, the larger the plant, the more noise it will be capable of making, and the more distinct and less frequent those sounds. Smaller plants are more likely to make a series of more subtle sounds that blend into each other, creating a soothing background music akin to white noise. Bamboos are among the best musical plants; their leaves make an especially good rattle, while smaller grasses make a more subtle and constant series of sounds. Take time out to spend in the garden, just listening, and try to work out which plants particular sounds are coming from. If you like a particular sound, and have singled out the plant producing it, you may want to think about how it might be possible to enhance it, or move it somewhere else in the garden.

left Perennials respond to the wind in various ways, from *Molinia caerulea* 'Transparent' (left) which is easily swayed by light breezes, to *Veronicastrum virginicum* (right) which only moves in stronger winds.

above *Panicum virgatum* 'Heavy Metal' is a good example of a seeded grass whose tiny heads capture movement particularly well. It flowers in late summer, and stands through the winter.

harmony

Under the soft light of cool, temperate climates, combinations of soft colours are usually harmonious. In climates where the light is stronger, such combinations would cease to be so effective because the light bleaches the colours. A sense of harmony can also result from certain combinations of plant forms, or leaf shapes, where there is a sense of everything working together, with no striking juxtapositions and nothing that gives the viewer a jolt.

A harmonious composition is not necessarily one that is relaxing. There is a fine line between a relaxed planting and a dull one, and without some contrast a planting will lack interest – one composed of too many sweet pinks and lavenders, for instance, might be cloying. You should be at ease in your garden, satisfied at a successful planting, but if a visitor relaxes too quickly then the garden does not offer enough stimulation! What is harmonious is a personal business, and one that is also culturally determined – some colour combinations in particular have been dependent upon the vagaries of fashion. So, when blending colour and shape, follow your own instincts and preferences.

In the picture to the left the combination of plants is undeniably harmonious. Related colours predominate: the pink and red of *Persicaria amplexicaulis* to the left, with the blue-mauve of *Perovskia atriplicifolia*, a mass of mauve origanum seedlings centre left and to the left the spires of *Digitalis ferruginea*. Notice, too, how the shapes of the persicaria and the perovskia flowerheads are roughly related, which promotes harmony. The colour of the digitalis does not mix so obviously with the others, but the flowers are so small that their colour is less important than the shape of the flowerhead. You can add interest and sparkle to a planting that is so well colour-coordinated that it is in danger of becoming boring simply by adding some softly coloured but dramatic shapes.

control

below In a park in Enköping, Sweden, large ornamental garlics (*Allium hollandicum* 'Purple Sensation') are striking plants for giving character to areas such as this which may be dull in late spring to early summer. They are easily planted to weave in and out of perennials which will flower later in the season, and will continue to flower every year. The use of bulbs such as this gets around a central problem of plantings dominated by a few species in which there is a lack of interest at certain times of the year.

Traditionally, the way in which plants were used in formal gardens was all about control: repeat or mass plantings of evergreens like yew or box were used to create a very disciplined effect. Control is about contrivance, about creating an effect which is quite artificial. It is about taking a plant usually grown in combination with other plants in a border and using it in such a way that it looks completely different: when you look at the salvias on the previous page, for example, your eye does not register their individual flower spikes, or even appreciate the separate plants, but sees only a solid mass. If you have enough space, you can use perennials in mass plantings too, but perhaps only for very special purposes, because there are definite disadvantages with this approach: the planting may look very dull once the flowers are over, for example, or problems in cultivation may lead to extensive gaps. Some perennials – grasses especially – create just such effects in the wild, and when they are used in this way in a garden or park the impression it offers is of a wild meadow or prairie. If you use more colourful flowering bulbs or

perennials in this way you will create a more dramatic effect; with rivers of strident colour flowing through a planting, the effect will also be more artificial.

One of the most effective ways of using a controlled planting is as a contrast to the complexities and intricacies of perennial borders, so that bold simplicity is seen as a fresh contrast. Formal features, as discussed on page 87, are commonly used, as is lawn, but the innovative might like to try using other plants with a long season of interest, such as grasses or evergreen perennials.

below left A sea of *Deschampsia cespitosa* 'Goldtau', with spires of *Digitalis ferruginea* emerging occasionally above the waves.

below right In a park in Enköping in central Sweden, a bold planting of salvias (*Salvia* x *sylvestris 'Rügen', Salvia nemorosa 'Ostfriesland'* and *Salvia* x *sylvestris 'Blauhügel'*) looks almost like a broad river, while the purple conjures up images of European moorland heather.

the sublime

above *Aster umbellatus* and *Helianthus salicifolius* are defined against *Eupatorium purpureum* 'Atropurpureum' and *Miscanthus sinensis* 'Malepartus'. The front of the border is filled with *Clematis* x *jouiniana* 'Praecox' (left) and *Sedum* 'Herbstfreude' (right).

next page *Persicaria polymorpha* (centre, rear) and *Eupatorium purpureum* 'Atropurpureum' dominate a late-summer border, with *Persicaria amplexicaulis* 'Firedance' (front), and *Foeniculum vulgare* (right). Grasses add interest to the bottom left.

The impression here is the opposite of control; nature seems to have escaped from the gardener. The lush growth of tall perennials and grasses seems to dwarf the human element as it evokes some of the most impressive natural habitats. This is a garden style for those who love nature; it is not for the faint-hearted, or for those who cling to traditional ideas of order.

'Sublime' is a word that is little used nowadays; perhaps it is due for a revival. It was much favoured by eighteenth-century English connoisseurs of landscape to describe scenery that was majestic and awe-inspiring: mountains, hills, white-water rivers and cascades. Historically, such scenery was regarded with disquiet, even horror; Dr Johnson drew the blinds of his coach to shut out the view as he travelled through parts of the Scottish Highlands. There are some plants that can inspire this range of emotions. Tall plants can be too overwhelming for timid gardeners who like everything to be tidy and neat, while those who appreciate raw nature, or have a real feeling for plants, will love the feeling that what they have created has actually taken over. The planting no longer feels part of them; it has a life of its own. Creating such a planting is all about 'controlled spontaneity'.

The best time to appreciate the sublime in the garden is late summer or early autumn, when big perennials, such as the North American Joe Pye weeds (*Eupatorium purpureum* group), ironweeds (*Vernonia* species) and grasses (many miscanthus) tower above you. Such plants grow at a very dramatic rate, many having not even emerged above ground level until late spring. Most tall perennials are from the American prairies, where the immensely rich flora forms a thick grassland – sometimes up to 2m (6½ft) high – so that walking in the prairie feels rather like being a midget in an ordinary meadow. You are overcome with a feeling of insignificance in the face of nature. It is equally possible to experience a similar feeling in marshland, among very tall reeds, and, of course, in woodland, and you can reproduce this overwhelming feeling in sublime perennial plantings by using perennials that grow to at least eye level. Moreover, you can enhance the feeling of the sublime by making a narrow pathway through a tall perennial planting, inviting the visitor actually to walk in among the plants, to be in the border, not just looking at it from outside. Tall hedges can generate a similar feeling, and you can exploit slopes too to create the same impression, because the height of the planting will be accentuated by the higher ground level, and the viewer will be forced to look up to see the plants. Those with small gardens should not feel excluded, for using large plants in such spaces is always the best option; small plants in a small garden will only make it feel smaller.

Eupatorium purpureum 'Atropurpureum' and the other Joe Pye weeds are the quintessential sublime perennials; some eupatoriums reach 3.5m (11½ft). They flower in late summer and their dull pink flowers are good for butterflies. *Artemisia lactiflora* 'Rosenschleier' flowers at this time too. This has pinky-white flowers with darker stems about 2m (6½ft) tall. With a bulkier look and large foliage are *Inula* species such as *I. magnifica* with its yellow daisies. *Silphium* species also have yellow flowers but are more graceful: their stems extend to 3–4m (10-13ft).

Some of the persicarias and related fallopias are notoriously invasive; not so *Persicaria polymorpha*, with cream flowers all summer on a perennial with a shrublike bulk. *Thalictrum* 'Elin', 3.5m (11½ft) high, also starts to flower early, inconspicuous white flowers atop single stems and elegant foliage, while *T. lucidum* is a soft yellow, 2.2m (7 ft) and their seedheads remain for the rest of the year.

Miscanthus grasses are mostly in the 2–3m (6½–10ft) range and are essential for creating a feeling of a prairie of marshland. Varieties should be chosen carefully for your region as some, particularly the taller ones like *M. floridulus,* need summer heat to flower and can be very late in cooler climes, while *Aster umbellatus* and violet *Aster novae-angliae* 'Violetta' are among the most valuable late-flowering tall perennials, along with the majestic veronias such as *V. crinita* 'Mammuth' which all have red-shot violet umbel-shaped flowerheads in early autumn.

mysticism

Mysticism in the garden depends almost entirely on circumstances which are beyond your control, when the power of the elements combines with nature – in the early morning, in fog, or at dusk, for instance – to make you feel quite alone. You cannot plant to create mysticism, but certain plants work best in mystical circumstances; they almost become people in your imagination, taking on human characteristics and attributes. You can imagine that they are looking at you or coming towards you.

Mysticism may seem a strange word to use with regard to a garden. It is best defined as a spiritual experience where one feels at one with the whole of creation, and hence at one with the divinity itself. The thirteenth-century German Dominican Meister Eckhart is one of the best-known Christian exponents of the same philosophy, while the Sufis of Islam are also familiar to many. By turning the conventional view of gardening upside down, however,

it is possible to create a vision of the garden which sees nature as supreme. The concept of the sublime has illustrated that it is possible to feel in awe of the garden, and it is only one step beyond this to see the garden as a paradigm of creation, and the human role within it as a minor one. Rather than controlling and taming nature, the gardener merely orchestrates living things that have their own rhythms and processes, over which he/she has little

above **The narrow spires of foxglove relative *Digitalis ferruginea* last a long time after their early summer flowering. They have an especially powerful presence in the garden. On the left is *Peucedanum verticillare.***

above **Umbellifers stand winter well, and in this case provide a good support for spider webs, often a strong and attractive element of an autumnal mood.**

control. The mystic wants to feel as though he is an integral part of nature, the expression of divine beauty, so the mystic's garden is somewhere very personal where it is possible to feel at one with nature – gardening as a spiritual exercise!

Gardens feel most mysterious and otherworldly, perhaps even most threatening, in fog, mist, drizzle, the attenuated light of dawn or dusk, perhaps even at night – moments when nature seems most in control. Thus, mysticism carries also a sense of the gothic, and the wild nature so beloved of the Romantic painters (e.g. Salvator Rosa) and poets (e.g. William Wordsworth). Think of the gothic imaginations of the Romantics whilst walking around the winter garden. Indeed, underlying its vision of nature as wild and unkempt, the nineteenth-century Romantic movement had a powerful sense of, and interest in, the mysterious and the spiritual.

Plants that evoke feelings of mystery and romance are often the same large species that evoke the sublime. Anything tall and upright that makes the subconscious think of a human form is highly effective in poor light: digitalis species (especially *D. ferruginea*), artichokes (*Cynara cardunculus*) and *Helianthus salicifolius*, for instance. Meanwhile, strong shapes and textures tend to stand out in fog; umbellifers are especially effective.

An acceptance of natural rhythms is also a part of acceptance of the supremacy of nature, that death and decay are part of life, for without their part in the eternal circle of rebirth there would be no material to feed the next generation. Tall dead stems in the garden, left to over-winter, can create an effective sight in winter weather. Acceptance of death is an important part of developing a relationship in the garden and decaying leaves have a role, and even sometimes a beauty of their own.

above **Fluffy plumes like this pink *Filipendula rubra* 'Venusta' accentuate the feelings engendered by this misty start to the day. The white plant is *Epilobium angustifolium* var. *album*.**

next page **The most resilient perennials stand through the winter to become the ghosts of the garden: *Digitalis ferruginea*, *Eryngium gigantea* and *Deschampsia cespitosa*.**

year-round planting

introduction

There is beauty to be found in nature on every single day of the year, so it must be possible to ensure that you have beauty in your garden all year round too. Those who see beauty only in bright colours, however, must learn to look differently at plants, at the forms and structures beneath.

Once you have learned to appreciate line and form, in browns and neutral tones, in stems, leaves and seedheads, it will become easier to see how it is possible to achieve the gardener's dream of 'a garden with year-round interest'. Creating something that gives this kind of satisfaction involves learning about natural processes and rhythms, and understanding how these affect different kinds of plants in a variety of habitats.

The importance of these natural cycles has already been acknowledged as vital to the planning gardener: pages 74–75 described how shade-tolerant woodland plants tend to flower early, how they are followed by woodland-edge species, and how it is only at the end of the summer that many of the largest sun-loving plants come into their own. Equally important to consider, however, is the fact that other plants that live in stressful environments tend to flower early; the relative lack of light in a wood is very stressful for a plant, for example. Plants from dry habitats need to flower, to seed and to grow early in the year, while the ground is still wet from the

winter's rain or snowmelt, and before the summer's heat, when they will often go into a kind of dormancy. This is why plants from drought-prone regions tend to flower in spring or early summer; many bulbs originally came from such areas. Plants from stress-free habitats, rich, fertile ground where there is plentiful water, need to fight for elbow room before they can indulge in flowering, so there is a strong tendency for wetland plants to flower later. Many of the best late-season border perennials have their ancestry in the moister parts of the American prairie, where soils are fertile and severe drought unlikely.

There are two elements to consider when you are organizing interest through the seasons: the first is to make the most of the temporary occurrences that have real impact, like flowering autumn colour, and the second is to create a sense of continuity by using more subtle, but long-lasting elements – exploiting foliage, for example. Particularly striking foliage, or even foliage that is simply a bit different, like the linear leaves of irises or grasses, is particularly useful when you are trying to link

the seasons in this way. Form is also vital for continuity, although with perennials form is in constant change, so that it combines continuity with a sense of progression.

Shrubs and woody plants, especially clipped evergreens, have traditionally been used for continuity, although too much reliance on evergreens results in a garden that can be boring. The woody bulk of a shrub is always there, whether it has leaves on it or not, and while it is this bulk that makes shrubs useful to gardeners, it is questionable how much space many gardens have for them. Bamboos are a useful alternative for continuity; they are evergreen, but have an elegant shape and tend to be vertical, taking up less space. Most bamboos do run however, and are best surrounded by an underground barrier (20–30cm/8–12in deep) to prevent spreading.

Perennials that peak relatively early but then maintain a distinguished appearance for much longer are especially worthy of attention. Veronicastrum virginicum, which produces its fine, vertically swept stems and flowers by early to midsummer, and keeps its statuesque good looks until well into the winter, is one such perennial. Monardas flower later in the year, but even after their colourful flowers have died they leave behind quite robust, whorled seedcases on upright stems for the winter. Some perennials have a strong structure for months before flowering, e.g. thistle relatives such as species of cirsium with their bold clumps of toothed leaves. This is why these

structural plants are so useful for seasonal continuity. In contrast, something like a cranesbill geranium, which flowers beautifully in early summer and then collapses into a sprawling mass of stems, has nothing like the same long-term appeal, although, to be fair, some geraniums do flower a second time later in the summer. Each garden is different, though; some plants in some regions tend to collapse after flowering, particularly in the autumn if it is wet. Very fertile soils also result in some plants becoming structurally weak. Packing plants in so that they hold each other up can be an effective way of preventing collapse – the geraniums just mentioned would be supported by grasses in their natural environment.

Grasses of course are vital for continuity. Evergreen species often contribute colours that are very different to the colours of traditional woody evergreens, while the taller species provide a slowly changing element for more than half the year and tend to stand inclement weather better than most flowering perennials.

There are things that make each season special, however, that mark them out for the gardener. As much as anything, these are a part of our collective cultural memory: bulbs in spring, along with fresh, young growth; bolder displays of flower in summer; seeds, fruits and russet colours in autumn. This chapter looks primarily at these special events, each characteristic of their time of year, in the context of linking nature and the garden.

above The experimental borders at the nursery in summer, autumn and winter, filled with the perennials and grasses that are fundamental to the new garden style. Although these are very functional beds – a plant collection – and not designed in the way that border plantings are, the overall impression is still the same. Here is an evocation of nature wrought by working with plants that are close to their wild ancestors.

The flowers of *Paeonia mlokosewitschii* (above) only appear in late spring, but its expanding young foliage (above right) offers exciting sculptural interest earlier in the season. The flowers are short-lived, but the elegant, rounded foliage continues to give pleasure until autumn. The yellow-green flower is that of *Bupleurum falcatum*,

a biennial umbellifer which thrives in similiar conditions to the peony, lightly shaded woodland-edge type habitats. As with foxgloves (*Digitalis*), its long-term survival in the garden depends upon self-seeding. Self-sowing plants like this often benefit from some occasional soil disturbance which provides them with new opportunities to grow.

Birth spring

Spring is a celebration of new life, or rebirth. Young growth is an equally vital part of spring; it can change dramatically from day to day so you will be richly rewarded for regular and frequent excursions into your garden at this time of the year. Many spring gardens are dominated by bulbs, with their remarkable ability to thrust forth their flowers almost as soon as they have burst above ground, but there are many perennials to consider too, especially as the season progresses. There are individual plants to appreciate, scattered among other, still-dormant species, and extensive drifts of species such as narcissi or crocuses too.

Many spring flowers have a long-lasting flowering season, so they often overlap with each other. Hellebores (below) are notable examples, partly because their petals do not drop but stay on the plant, gradually changing colour, while ground-covering *Phlox divaricata* 'Clouds of Perfume' (below, shown with hellebores), meanwhile, provides a bolder, but shorter splash of colour at the end of spring.

late spring

By late spring an increasing number of perennials have come into flower, especially the larger ones, so the garden begins to lose the sparse feel of early spring, and looks fuller. Most spring-flowering perennials do not – unlike bulbs – become dormant, so they are unable to protect themselves against dry summer conditions. As a result most prefer cool situations, in humus-rich soil (similar to the leafmould of woodlands) which, while being well-drained, does not dry out. In these cool temperatures flowers stay fresher for longer, which explains why the flowering season of spring flowers is quite often an extended one. In climates where springs are short and sharp, on the other hand, this may not be the case.

Watching new growth unfurl is one of the joys of spring: the croziers of ferns such as *Polystichum setiferum* 'Ringens' (above left) are fascinating to behold. Meanwhile, some plants are so keen to flower that their leaves have to wait their turn. One such is *Podophyllum hexandrum* 'Majus', pictured opposite with *Dicentra formosa* which, with its long flowering season, is one of those perennials that acts as a link between spring and early summer. The sweet-scented lavender flowers of *Lunaria rediviva* (above and in detail, left) form a soft colour contrast with lime-green *Smyrnium perfoliatum* in a lightly shaded area. The smyrnium dies after flowering, while the lunaria's 'looking-glass' seedcases provide interest later in the year.

Life early summer

Early summer is the season when a wide variety of perennials burst into flower. Most of them are low-growing or clump-forming in contrast to the later-flowering species, which tend to be more erect in their growth. Many of these early species are from woodland-edge habitats; they thrive in light shade, though often in full sun as well. Hardy geraniums, or cranesbills, are a most useful group; the bright pink *Geranium psilostemon* (above) is one of the largest and brightest. Their role as ground-cover plants, suppressing weeds, makes them popular with many gardeners, and there is now a very large number of both species and hybrids available. A few taller plants, like digitalis, the foxglove group, are valuable for providing an element of contrasting form.

Bold-leaved foliage plants like hostas will provide continuity, a constant in plantings where change is the norm. Indeed, hostas are one of the finest groups of foliage perennials, and wonderful companions for early-summer flowers. For example, the blue-grey *Hosta* 'Halcyon' forms a gentle backdrop here (above) for a bright pink *Paeonia officinalis*, the dark red flowers of *Astrantia major* 'Ruby Wedding' and the green-flowered spikes of *Heuchera* 'Greenfinch'. Although they prefer a moist site, hostas will nevertheless flourish in most soils as long as they receive some shade – conditions which suit astrantias and heucheras too. Heucheras are an increasingly important group of clump-forming plants, with less need for moisture than hostas, and less prone to slug damage.

midsummer

Some of the most colourful early to midsummer-flowering plants come originally from dry habitats, where summer drought can curtail growth and the speed of the seed production/dissemination cycle is accelerated. In moister garden conditions the red-pink *Centranthus ruber* and both the varieties of salvia species with it (above), can have a longer flowering season.

It is midsummer that brings the really magnificent range of taller perennials that make the rest of the warm months such a rewarding season for gardeners. And at ground level any bare ground in the border should now have disappeared beneath a solid mass of perennial growth. Most of the species flowering here are, once again, noticeably taller than those that flowered in early summer: monardas are among the most rewarding. The scarlet *Monarda* 'Squaw' is pictured here, alongside *Clematis viticella* 'Rubra Grandiflora' – another striking red. The later-flowering *Clematis viticella* varieties have smaller flowers and hence far more elegance than the more common large-flowered hybrids, which have lost their natural sense of proportion.

Verbena bonariensis, meanwhile, in the foreground to the left, is a most useful perennial. It has a 'transparent' quality, as well as one of the longest flowering seasons, often continuing to produce its mauve flowers until the first frosts mark the onset of autumn. This and the related *Verbena hastata* almost inevitably self-sow, scattering themselves around the border, a valuable attribute as they take up little space.

Late summer is the climax of the year for perennials and for those who love them. Many of those that flower now grow large and lush; some even grow tall enough to dwarf a human. *Eupatorium purpureum* 'Atropurpureum' (top left) towers above the pink flowers of *Lavatera cachemiriana* (left), a monarda (centre), a lythrum (upper right) and achilleas (right) in the border on the left. Most of the plants that flower at this time are strongly structural plants with an upright habit. They leave minimal space, so there is little need for filler plants, but one that is useful is *Saponaria lempergii* 'Max Frei' (bottom left) which can play an important role at the front of the border. In the picture above, a eupatorium still stands majestically although it has finished flowering – it is strong enough to stand all winter. In front of it is the tall stem of *Helianthus salicifolius*, a perennial sunflower, not grown for its flowers, but for its fine leaves radiating out from the tall stem – an unusual foliage plant, which works well near the front of large borders. Accompanying them is the long-flowering *Verbena bonariensis*, whose flowers provide a useful link between midsummer and early winter.

Death early autumn

While early autumn is very much a continuation of the splendour of late summer, as time moves on increasing numbers of flowers die, and the stems of plants that continue to flower become straggly or ragged and grasses play an increasingly important role in the garden. Many grasses, the big miscanthus varieties in particular, do not even flower until quite late. They will become more and more important in the border because, as the perennials finish flowering, die and begin to collapse, their seedheads ripen and become a more dominant visual feature. In the picture on the left, for example, *Molinia caerulea* 'Transparent' forms a delicate backdrop for late-flowering perennials, including *Sanguisorba officinalis* 'Asiatic Form', with its dark red buttons and *Echinacea purpurea*. The number of seedheads multiplies, but this should be seen as a positive development, as some flowers look their best as they 'go over': the heads of *Echinacea purpurea* (lower left), for example, are characterized by a decadent beauty as they wilt. The seedheads of *Veronicastrum* var. *sibiricum* 'Spring Dew' (above) continue to look striking, creating a dramatic contrast with the russet *Helenium* 'Kupferzwerg'. The seedheads of *Epilobium angustifolium* var. *album* are more spectacular, forming great clouds of fluffy white.

Plants that die well: *Aster, Aconitum, Anemone japonica* hybrids, *Cimicifuga simplex, Helenium autumnale* hybrids, *Kirengeshoma palmata, Persicaria amplexic*

idbeckia, *Scutellaria incana*, *Sedum telephium* cultivars, *Solidago* cultivars, *Tricyrtis formosana*, *Verbesina alternifolia*, Grasses: *Miscanthus*, *Molinia* cultivars

mid-autumn

The balance tips now – away from flowers and life, to seed, dying foliage, and death – though there is still a promise of eventual rebirth and resurrection. Evergreens play an increasingly important role in the garden, a strong, dark counterpoint to the dominant brown and straw yellow tones. Some flowers remain (above), including *Astrantia major* 'Roma' and *Saponaria lempergii* 'Max Frei', but already the *Geranium soboliferum* and *G. wlassovianum* (detail left) and a molinia grass on the right carry the rich tints of autumn. The autumn colours of the trees are matched by only a few perennials, among them certain geraniums, *Euphorbia palustre*, *Darmera peltata* and *Gaura lindheimeri*. Grasses combine with *Darmera peltata* to form a picture of autumnal decay, underlining the solid shapes of the hedge and the clipped yews (above right), while the light from the low sun picks out the shapes and colours of *Eryngium giganteum* (below right). These are among the stiffest perennial remains; they stay standing even after months of wet and windy weather, when everything about them has gone soggy and collapsed.

late autumn

Many gardeners see the dead and dying stems of perennials at the end of the year as rubbish to clear away. Plants can be beautiful in death as well as in life, however – some might argue that a plant is not worth growing unless it looks good when it is dead! Many species do indeed continue to look good after life has ceased to flow through their veins, especially in late autumn when the subtle straw tones of their stems and leaves are still fresh. Moreover, countless seedheads begin to appear among the dying stems and foliage – each one as distinctive as the flower from which it grew – so it is worth taking the time to walk around the late-autumn border, to appreciate these and to watch summer's flowers turn from the embodiment of colour and growth into sculpture and nemesis. The seedheads of *Eupatorium maculatum* (above top) are firmly clustered, while those of *Ligularia japonica* (above) have been designed to be blown away on the breeze. A big *Miscanthus sinensis* 'Flamingo' grass dominates a planting (right), and its silvery heads will remain for much of the winter, while the seedheads of the flowers in front will soon disintegrate, leaving behind skeletal shapes such as those pictured above. A few flowers of *Persicaria amplexicaulis* remain among the autumn colours here; this species will flower until the frosts become too sharp and frequent, when it will dramatically collapse.

Plants that will stand through winter: *Achillea, Agastache, Amsonia, Astilbe, Cimicifuga simplex* and cultivars, *Echinacea, Eryngium, Eupatorium purpureum 'Atro*

winter

Frosts and snow, particularly hoar frosts, which cover every surface with a layer of ice crystals, can transform the browns of autumn into a grey and white wonderland. *Miscanthus sinensis* 'Silberturm', its seedheads weighed down by frost, makes a fountain of ice (left), while the resilient heads of the stiffer monardas stand in front. On the right are *Verbena hastata* (above) and *Eryngium giganteum* (below).

The weather plays a vital role in the appearance of perennials in the winter. If the autumn is dry, dead foliage will stand upright, ideal for dramatic effects when the hoar frosts come. Wet autumns will cause many perennials to become soggy or to collapse. Only a few will remain: those, like monardas and phlomis, that have stiff stems and tight seedheads, and grasses which generally stand and look good through the winter. A gardener who clears away dying perennials in the autumn will not experience any of this.

um', *Monarda*, *Nepeta* species, *Phlomis* species, *Rodgersia*, *Rudbeckia*, *Sedum* cultivars; Grasses: *Calamagrostis brachytricha*, *Deschampsia cespitosa*

plant directory

This is a listing of key plants, the most important perennials and grasses. Each plant is described and cultivation notes and suitable plant combinations supplied. Not all plants listed in the combinations are described here, but will readily be found in most reference books.

perennials

ACANTHUS
These are dramatic perennials used for their architectural character.

hungaricus
A tall, bushy, ornamental plant with shiny green, serrated leaves. The large flowers, which appear in midsummer, are white and mauve, reminiscent of foxgloves from a distance. H1m x S60cm (3½ x 2ft).

CULTIVATION These plants tolerate dry conditions well. Place in sun or light shade.
COMBINATIONS Heuchera, Geranium.

ACHILLEA   YARROW
These are upright perennials with fern-like foliage, producing large, usually flat, umbel-like flowerheads in summer.

millefolium
Flat heads of off-white flowers open during mid- to late summer, with a second flowering if deadheaded. The foliage is very well defined and dark green. H75 x S45cm (2½ x 1½ft).

HYBRIDS
'Credo'
This new cultivar is not rampant like A. millefolium. The sulphur-yellow blooms make good cut flowers. H1.2m x S45cm (4 x 1½ft).

'Feuerland'
Bright red flowers with yellow hearts which fade with age to a rich shade of yellow ochre. H75 x S45cm (2½ x 1½ft).

'Martina'
A sturdy plant that produces large, sulphur-yellow flowerheads over a lengthy season. H60 x S30cm (2 x 1ft).

'Summerwine'
The florets are deep red-wine colour, later turning purple. H75 x S45cm (2½ x 1½ft).

'Terracotta'
Flowers that vary in colour from yellow to light orange-brown. H90 x S45 cm (3 x 1½ft).

'Walther Funcke'
A smaller version of 'Feuerland' with red ochre flowers and a greyer, slightly coarser leaf. H75 x S30cm (2½ x 1ft).

CULTIVATION These very resilient plants can self-seed vigorously. They prefer well-drained soil and sun.
COMBINATIONS Artemisia, Eryngium, Filipendula, Gypsophila, Monarda, Salvia, Scabiosa, Stipa, Veronicastrum.

ACONITUM
Perennials with their flowers in spires.

carmichaelli Wilsonii Group
A tall attractive background plant, striking for its blue flowers in autumn when there is little real blue in the garden. H120 x S30cm (4 x 1ft).

cammarum 'Grandiflorum Album'
The buds have a green glow and are pure white when open. H120 x S30cm (4 x 1ft).

'Newry Blue'
A sturdy plant, one of the first to flower in early summer, with dark blue leaves. H1.2 x S30cm (4 x 1ft).

CULTIVATION Full sun or light shade, with the best results in a fertile, never dry soil.
COMBINATIONS Astilbe, Anemone, Cimicifuga, Thalictrum.

AGASTACHE
Perennials with aromatic leaves and spires of flowers in summer.

foeniculum
Violet-blue flowers that are attractive to bees and smell strongly of aniseed appear in mid- to late summer. H90 x S30 cm (3 x 1ft).

CULTIVATION They enjoy sun and thrive in any type of soil.
COMBINATIONS Achillea, Anthemis, Artemisia, Eryngium, Knautia.

AMSONIA
These slow-growing, clump-forming perennials produce umbel-like clusters of funnel-shaped flowers in early summer.

orientalis (SYN. RHAZYA ORIENTALIS)
Soft grey-blue flowers are borne in loose clusters. This species is best used as a filler, preferably in a sunny position. H30 x S30cm (1 x 1ft).

tabernaemontana var. salicifolia
The young stems are purple-black in stark contrast to willowy foliage. Clusters of blue flowers appear in midsummer. H75 x S30cm (2½ x 1ft).

CULTIVATION Amsonias like well-drained soil in a semi-shaded position, but leave them alone once planted as they hate disturbance.
COMBINATIONS Achillea, Astrantia, Eryngium, Euphorbia, Filipendula, Geranium, Geum, Hemerocallis, Heuchera, Hosta, Salvia.

ANEMONE   WINDFLOWER
The herbaceous anemones have disc-shaped flowers which open in late summer and autumn.

X HYBRIDA   JAPANESE ANEMONES
Superb plants with pink flowers carried on abundant stalks from late summer through to early autumn. H1.5m x S60cm (5 x 2ft).

CULTIVATION Japanese anemones thrive in humus-rich, well-drained soil, in full sun or semi-shade.
COMBINATIONS Aconitum, Cimicifuga, Eupatorium, Persicaria, Verbena.

ANGELICA
Architectural perennials whose short-lived summer flowers are carried in umbels.

gigas
This develops into a very striking plant with dark plum, dome-shaped flowerheads opening in late summer. H1.4m x S45cm (4½ x 1½ft).

'Vicar's Mead'
The flowers and seedheads are purple-pink, held in open umbels above the reddish leaves. H1.4m x S45cm (4½ x 1½ft).

CULTIVATION Angelicas tolerate any soil but require full sun. Easy to grow from seed.
COMBINATIONS Eupatorium, Monarda, Persicaria, Phlox.

ANTHRISCUS
Small flowers are arranged in umbels and open in early summer.

sylvestris 'Ravenswing'
This is a form of cow parsley with erect stems and white umbels emerging from between the fern-like, dark red-brown leaves in late spring. H75 x S30 cm (2½ x 1ft).

CULTIVATION Likes to be in sun or part-shade, in any fertile soil that is not too dry.
COMBINATIONS Aquilegia, Chaerophyllum, Digitalis, Nepeta, Sanguisorba.

ARALIA
Large perennials with masses of flowers carried in large plumes. Aralias are also grown for their bold leaves.

californica
Plumes of white flowers in mid- to late summer are followed by clusters of black berries. The elegant, light green, divided leaves continue to expand throughout the summer. H2.5 x S2m (8 x 6½ft).

CULTIVATION Although fully hardy it needs some shelter. Does best in a fertile, well-drained soil, in sun or semi-shade.
COMBINATIONS Calamagrostis, Cimicifuga, Ligularia, Macleaya, Miscanthus, Rodgersia.

ARTEMISIA   MUGWORT, WORMWOOD
Most artemisias are cultivated for their foliage which is often silvery and aromatic. However, A. lactiflora (white mugwort) is exceptional in being grown for its plumes of cream flowers as well as for its dark green, deeply cut leaves.

lactiflora Guizhou Group
Produces creamy flowers on arching stems during late summer and the beginning of autumn. Shaggy leaves are purple when young. H1.8m x S75cm (6 x 2½ft).

lactiflora 'Rosenschleier'

Dull pink flowers make a dramatic contrast to very dark red stems. Grows up to H2m x S75cm (6½ x 2½ft).

CULTIVATION These artemisias appreciate moist soil in sun or part-shade.
COMBINATIONS Achillea, Anthemis, Eryngium, Knautia, Perovskia, Platycodon, Salvia.

ASTER

Genus of perennials grown for their persistent daisy flowerheads produced over a long season from summer into autumn.

cordifolius 'Little Carlow'

A mass of elegant, tiny violet-blue flowers appear in late summer and early autumn. H90 x 45cm (3 x 1½ft).

cordifolius 'Silver Spray'

Tiny translucent flowers of silvery blue to white, with reddening hearts, appear in late summer and early autumn. H1.2m x S45cm (4 x 1½ft).

x frikartii 'Mönch'

Violet-blue flowers with yellow centres are produced without interruption from summer until late autumn. H75 x S45cm (2½ x 1½ft).

lateriflorus 'Coombe Fishacre'

A mass of lilac flowers with red centres smother this bushy plant from summer to early autumn. H90 x S45 cm (3 x 1½ft).

lateriflorus 'Horizontalis'

The dark leaves provide a good background to the small white flowers, with red-brown hearts, which appears in late summer. This is a bushy plant with spreading growth. H60 x S60cm (2 x 2ft).

lateriflorus 'Lady in Black'

A mass of charming, soft beige-pink flowers open from late summer to early autumn. The stems and leaves are purple on this tall cultivar. H1.4m x S75cm (4 x 2½ft).

novae-angliae 'Violetta'

A New England aster that bears striking deep purple flowers with yellow hearts, opening from late summer to early autumn. H1.5m x S60cm (5 x 2ft).

umbellatus

Attractive little white flowers in late summer and early autumn are borne on sturdy, upright stems, branching and flattened at the top. Allow the striking white seedheads to develop in winter. H1.8m x S75cm (6 x 2½ft).

HYBRID CULTIVARS
'Herfstweelde'

Flowers of pale blue with yellow centres – as fine as those of *Aster ericoides* but twice the size – appear from late summer and until early winter. H1.4m x S75cm (4½ x 2½ft).

'Pink Star'

Good pink flowers, from midsummer to autumn, are carried on a sturdy, upright, border plant. H1.2m x S60cm (6 x 2ft).

'Twilight'

Small daisy-like blue flowers produced in abundance from midsummer to autumn. This begins to flower earlier than other forms of aster and has a slowly spreading habit. H60 x S45cm (2 x 1½ft).

CULTIVATION These all like well-drained soil with adequate moisture throughout the year, preferably in sun or partial shade.
COMBINATIONS Achillea, Calamagrostis, Cimcifuga, Echinacea, Eupatorium, Helenium, Lobelia, Nepeta, Veronicastrum.

ASTILBE

Summer-flowering perennials that are grown for their soft plumes of flowers.

chinensis var. taquetii 'Purpurlanze'

Purple-red flowers open in midsummer and, if left, faded flowerheads retain an ornamental quality deep into winter. H90 x S75cm (3 x 2½ft).

'Professor van der Wielen' (thunbergii hybrid)

Elegant white flowerheads in late summer look striking, especially when planted in large groups. H1.2m x S90cm (4 x 3ft).

CULTIVATION All astilbes like humus-rich, moisture-retaining soil and shade.
COMBINATIONS Astrantia, Campanula, Delphinium, Digitalis, Geranium, Hemerocallis, Heuchera. Most grasses.

ASTILBOIDES

Dramatic, large-leaved perennials, with arching panicles of white flowers, are well suited to waterside habitats.

tabularis (SYN. RODGERSIA TABULARIS)

Panicles of white flowers in midsummer rise above the strikingly large, circular leaves. This is still widely sold under its old name. H1.2m x S75cm (4 x 2½ft).

CULTIVATION Grow in sun or partial shade, but plants do not like too dry a soil.
COMBINATIONS Astrantia, Cimicifuga, Deschampsia, Geranium, Hemerocallis, Hosta, Iris, Lythrum, Molinia, Thalictrum.

ASTRANTIA HATTIE'S PINCUSHION, MASTERWORT

With flowers in button-like miniature umbels, these provide midsummer floral interest.

major 'Canneman'

This cultivar tends to be variable as it is reproduced from seed. The large, dark red blooms fade to green or white and flower often two or three times a year, from late spring to autumn. H75 x S30cm (2½ x 1ft).

major 'Claret'

This is a seedling of the popular 'Ruby Wedding' and the darkest of all the astrantias. It bears red flowers on wiry, branched stems in early summer. H75 x S30cm (2½ x 1ft).

major 'Roma'

This is a good pink variety, flowering from late spring. H75 x S30cm (2½ x 1ft).

major subsp. involucrata 'Shaggy'

Also sold under the name 'Margery Fish'. Flowerheads develop long, twisted white bracts with shaded green tips in late spring. H75 x S30cm (2½ x 1ft).

maxima

Large, pure pink flowers in midsummer emerge from among the three-lobed, serrated leaves (*A. major* and its varieties have five lobes). H60 x S45cm (2 x 1½ft).

CULTIVATION Masterworts tolerate sun or partial shade, and require soil that is well-drained but never dry.
COMBINATIONS Achillea, Astilbe, Eryngium, Foeniculum, Lychnis, Lythrum, Sesleria.

BAPTISIA

Distinguished-looking perennials with pea flowers, often with a shrubby appearance.

australis

Sturdy grey-green stems and blue-grey flowers make this plant attractive even when it is not flowering as the lupin-shaped flowers are succeeded by ornamental seedheads. H1.2m x S60cm (4 x 2ft).

pendula (SYN B.ALBA)

This species is known as the white couterpart of *B. australis* with white flowers contrasting with filmy greyish stalks. Just a lone specimen can be attractive. H90 x S60cm (3 x 2ft).

CULTIVATION Needs sun and fertile soil. Can be slow to establish and should not be moved once planted.
COMBINATIONS Centaurea, Crambe, Delphinium, Papaver.

CALAMINTHA CALAMINT

Useful as filler plants, calamints have a low, bushy habit and aromatic leaves.

grandiflora

Long-lasting flowers of an easily combined pink are produced from early spring until late summer. H35 x S20cm (1–1½ft x 8in).

nepeta subspecies nepeta
LESSER CALAMINT

Porcelain-blue flowers open in midsummer and continue till autumn. H30 x S20cm (1ft x 8in).

nepeta subsp. glandulosa 'White Cloud'

The white flowers last from midsummer until autumn. H30 x S20 cm (1ft x 8in).

CULTIVATION Calamints like full sun and tolerate dry conditions; in fact, they are happy in any soil.
COMBINATIONS Achillea, Centranthus, Coreopsis, Gypsophila, Monarda, Saponaria, Sidalcea.

CAMPANULA BELLFLOWER

Spring- and summer-flowering perennials that are best regarded as filler plants, although *C. latifolia* has definite upright structure. Fflowers are generally mauve-blue and bell-shaped, sometimes in clusters.

iflora MILKY BELLFLOWER

f all the tall campanulas *C. lactiflora* has the smallest flowers. These vary from pale to dark blue, lightening towards the centre, and appear in midsummer. Cutting back in mid-May delays flowering and also prevents the plant from growing too tall and falling over. H1.5m x S45cm (5 x 1½ft).

lactiflora 'Alba'
This white-flowered version of the milky bellflower also blooms in midsummer. H1.2m x S30cm (6 x 1ft).

lactiflora 'Loddon Anna'
Light, lilac-pink flowers open in midsummer. H1.5m x S30cm (5 x 1ft).

latifolia 'Gloaming'
Lilac-pink flowers in midsummer are followed by delicate filigree seedheads well into winter. H75 x S30cm (2½ x 1ft).

portenschlagiana DALMATIAN BELLFLOWER
Very small plants that produce purple-blue bell-shaped flowers in abundance in midsummer. H20 x S45cm (8in x 1½ft).

poscharskyana 'E.H. Frost'
Small, bell-shaped flowers of pale blue to white with darker centres are borne on the end of twisted stems in early summer. H20 x S45cm (8in x 1½ft).

poscharskyana 'Lisduggan Variety'
Lilac-pink flowers in early summer create good groundcover. H20 x S45cm (8in x 1½ft).

CULTIVATION Fully hardy and suits sun or partial shade, but colour is best in shade.
COMBINATIONS Alchemilla, Astilbe, Astrantia, Filipendula, Geum, Lychnis.

CENTAUREA KNAPWEED
Genus characterized by thistle-like flowerheads that look like buttons in the middle distance.

montana 'Carnea'
Good overall effect in early summer is the result of a combination of pale lilac flowers, with lilac-red centres and showy stamens, and grey leaves. H45 x S30cm (1½ x 1ft).

CENTRANTHUS VALERIAN
Perennials with tight flowerheads make good filler plants for dry, rocky places.

ruber 'Albus'
Heads of countless white flowers in midsummer appear among leaves with a filmy blue bloom. Use the airy, white inflorescences to forge links between stiff groups of plants. H60 x S60cm (2 x 2ft).

ruber var. coccineus
Red flowers in midsummer lend a vigorous accent to a border. H60 x S60cm (2 x 2ft).

CULTIVATION Valerians thrive in sun and poor soil.
COMBINATIONS Achillea, Artemisia, Astrantia, Monarda, Penstemon, Potentilla, Salvia, Sidalcea, Stipa, Veronicastrum.

CHAEROPHYLLUM
Umbellifers, but these are more reliably perennial than most of the family.

hirsutum 'Roseum'
Umbels of pink flowers open in late spring. H90 x S45cm (3 x 1½ft).

CULTIVATION These like sun or partial shade and are tolerant of any soil.
COMBINATIONS Alchemilla, Astrantia, Geranium, Geum, Luzula, Salvia, Veronica.

CIMICIFUGA BUGBANE
A genus characterized by imposing spires of flowers in late summer and autumn.

simplex
Decorative white flower spikes appear in autumn. This species has the most attractive spring growth of all bugbanes and retains a good silhouette well into winter. H1.4m x S75cm (4½ x 2½ft).

simplex Atropurpurea Group
White, sweetly fragranced flowers appear in late summer, tinged at the outer edges by the same purple-red of the stems. H1.8m x S75cm (6 x 2½ft).

CULTIVATION Bugbanes like light shade and dislike hot or dry positions. They are happy in moist, well-drained soil.
COMBINATIONS Aconitum, Anemone, Aster, Astilbe, Lobelia, Persicaria, Sanguisorba, Veronicastrum.

CLEMATIS
Mostly climbers, but self-supporting or small-growing clematis can be filler plants.

integrifolia
Superb purple-blue flowers with cream hearts in early summer are followed by fluffy seeds that remain on the plant until late autumn. Treat this as a border perennial. H60 x S75cm (2 x 2½ft).

recta
Wonderful little white flowers in summer, followed by silvery seedheads that last into autumn. Its stems shoot 2m (6½ft) into the air when in season and need some support. H2 x 1.4m (6½ x 4½ft).

CULTIVATION Both species thrive in sunny positions, in any well-drained soil.
COMBINATIONS Astrantia, Crambe, Eryngium

COREOPSIS TICKSEED
This genus is characterized by daisy-like flowerheads.

tripteris
Clusters of tiny yellow flowers on slender stalks open in late summer. H2m x S75cm (6½ x 2½ft).

CULTIVATION Tickseeds need full sun and well-drained, fertile soil.
COMBINATIONS Astilbe, Delphinium, Eryngium, Filipendula, Phlox, Thalictrum.

CRAMBE
Plants produce big displays of flowers in umbel-like heads amid bold leaves.

cordifolia
Similar to *C. maritima*, it forms a dramatic summer screen of creamy white when in flower. H60 x S60cm (2 x 2ft).

maritima SEA KALE
Globular clusters of white blossom appear in summer above the large, waxy blue-grey leaves. H60 x S60cm (2 x 2ft).

CULTIVATION These prefer sun but tolerate some shade and thrive in well-drained soil.
COMBINATIONS Baptisia, Delphinium, Hemerocallis, Papaver, Rheum.

DIGITALIS FOXGLOVE
Perennials and biennials that are grown for their spikes or spires of flowers.

ferruginea RUSTY FOXGLOVE
Small, brown-veined, copper yellow flowers held in narrow spikes appear in summer on a tall, slender plant that self-seeds freely. H1.2m x S20cm (4ft x 8in).

grandiflora YELLOW FOXGLOVE
Big, creamy yellow flowers with light brown veins open over a long period in summer. H60 x S20cm (2ft x 8in).

parviflora
An unusual plant laden with small brown flowers in summer. H60 x S20cm (2ft x 8in).

CULTIVATION Foxgloves do best in semi-shade and moist, well-drained soil. They usually self-seed well.
COMBINATIONS Astrantia, Campanula, Eryngium, Euphorbia, Geranium, Heuchera.

ECHINACEA CONEFLOWER
Large daisy flowers on sturdy plants that flower mid-to late summer.

purpurea 'Augustkönigin'
Large daisy-like, purple-pink flowers atop long, robust stems in midsummer. The cone-shaped hearts of the flowerheads are suffused with a deep orange glow. Particularly attractive to butterflies and bees. H90 x S45cm (3 x 1½ft).

purpurea 'Green Edge'
This has attractive white flowers with a touch of green in the petals. H1m x S50cm (3½ x 1¾ft).

purpurea 'Magnus'
This has flat-lying pink-purple petals which are slightly reflexed. H1m x S50cm (3½ x 1¾ft).

purpurea 'Rubinstern'
The flowers are redder and more expressive here than those of the species. H1m x S50cm (3½ x 1¾ft).

CULTIVATION Full sun and fertile soil.
COMBINATIONS Aster, Eupatorium, Filipendula, Helenium, Lythrum, Phlox, Persicaria, Sanguisorba.

ECHINOPS GLOBE THISTLE
Summer-flowering perennials that are grown for their globe-like flowerheads.

ritro 'Veitch's Blue'

Ball-like purple-blue flowers on long, robust stems appear amid grey-green leaves in midsummer. H1.2m x S75cm (4 x 2½ft).

sphaerocephalus

The large, white, midsummer flowers are favoured by bees and butterflies. This is a densely branched plant with a superb winter silhouette. H1.4m x S90cm (4½ x 3ft).

CULTIVATION Echinops do best in full sun and poor soil.
COMBINATIONS Achillea, Geranium, Perovskia, Salvia, Sanguisorba, Veronicastrum.

EPILOBIUM   (SYN. CHAMERION)
Flowers in spires in early to mid summer.

angustifolium var. album

Seen from a distance, this plant looks like a very fine type of larkspur but a close glance reveals the pure white form of the well-known willow herb. H1.5m x 60cm (5 x 2ft).

CULTIVATION Needs sun and suits most soils. It does not seed, but the roots can still run.
COMBINATIONS Delphinium, Filipendula, Lychnis, Sanguisorba, Thalictrum.

ERYNGIUM   ERYNGO, SEA HOLLY
Very structural plants with tight flowerheads that look like buttons or thimbles and resemble thistles, though they are unrelated.

alpinum 'Blue Star'

Steely blue bracts surround cylindrical blue flowerheads which open in midsummer. H75 x S30cm (2½ x 1ft).

giganteum 'MISS WILLMOTT'S GHOST'

Steely grey flowers appear amid silver-grey leaves from mid- to late summer. This is biennial, but self-seeds well. H90 x S45cm (3 x 1½ft)

x tripartitum

A mass of purple-blue flowerheads open on densely branched stems from midsummer to early autumn. H90 x S60cm (3 x 2ft).

CULTIVATION Sea hollies do best in sun and a fertile, well-drained soil.
COMBINATIONS Achillea, Dictamnus, Lychnis, Phlomis, Potentilla, Salvia.

EUPATORIUM   HEMP AGRIMONY
These possess an architectural quality, emphasized by their foliage and umbel-like heads of softly coloured flowers.

cannabinum Flore Pleno

Striking, old-fashioned pink flowers that last from midsummer to autumn. H1.5m x S90cm (5 x 3ft).

purpureum subspecies maculatum 'Album'

Smaller white flower clusters appear in late summer. H2.5m x S90cm (8 x 3ft).

purpureum subspecies maculatum 'Atropurpureum'

Large umbel-like clusters of small purple-pink flowers in late summer attract bees and butterflies. H1.5m x S90cm (5 x 3ft).

CULTIVATION These stately plants prefer sun or partial shade and moist, well-drained soil.
COMBINATIONS Angelica, Cimicifuga, Echinacea, Helenium, Miscanthus, Persicaria, Verbena, Veronicastrum.

EUPHORBIA   SPURGE
The cup-shaped bracts enclose several flowers that lack typical sepals and petals. Most spurges are fillers although *E. characias* has a strong structure.

characias subspecies wulfenii

Small yellow-green flowers with very obvious dark eyes appear on numerous stems in late spring. Plants have a bushy and rounded habit. H90 x S90cm (3 x 3ft).

dulcis 'Chameleon'

Yellow-green flowers open in early summer. In sunny positions the leaves turn from green to purple and appear transparent red. H45 x S45cm (1½ x 1½ft).

griffithii 'Dixter'

One of the most striking plants of early summer, when the bright orange flowers and bracts contrast well against the narrow, red leaves. H75 x S45cm (2½ x 1½ft).

schillingii

Branched yellow-green flowers open in early summer. The young shoots appear transparent red and the olive-green leaves have white veining. H1.2m x S45cm (4ft x 1½ft).

CULTIVATION Spurges grow best in sun or partial shade, in moist well-drained soil.
COMBINATIONS Actaea, Astrantia, Campanula, Digitalis, Epimedium, Hosta, Lamium.

FILIPENDULA
Summer-flowering perennials bear flowers in plumes.

purpurea 'Nephele'

Pinkish flowers appear in midsummer. H1.2cm x S45cm (4 x 1½ft).

rubra 'Venusta'

A spreading plant with large, bright pink, flower trusses in midsummer that fade to a good chestnut brown. H1.8m x S75 cm (6 x 2½ft).

CULTIVATION These do best in full sun and water-retentive soil.
COMBINATIONS Achillea, Echinacea, Echinops, Miscanthus, Monarda, Phlox, Sanguisorba, Thalictrum, Verbena.

FOENICULUM   FENNEL
Perennials grown for their umbels of yellow flowers and scented leaves.

vulgare 'Giant Bronze'

Soft yellow flowers appear in midsummer in dramatic combination with the ultra-fine bronze-coloured leaves. H1.5m x S75cm (5 x 2½ft).

CULTIVATION Fennel grows best in sunny, open sites and tolerates dry conditions. It may die after flowering, especially on wet soils, but usually self-seeds well.
COMBINATIONS Calamagrostis, Echinacea, Echinops, Lavatera, Monarda, Sanguisorba, Stipa, Verbascum, Veronicastrum.

GALEGA   GOAT'S RUE
Summer-flowering perennials that bear their flowers in spires.

orientalis

Fine clusters of bright blue flowers appear without interruption from midsummer until early autumn. Plants have a strong tendency to spread. H1.2m x S90cm (4 x 3ft).

CULTIVATION Grow in any open sunny position, in well-drained soil.
COMBINATIONS Delphinium, Eryngium, Euphorbia, Filipendula, Lychnis, Salvia.

GAURA
Filler plants with flowers borne on long, bending stems which become structural in autumn, when the leaf colour is also good.

lindheimeri 'Whirling Butterflies'

White flowers appear in mid- to late summer. H90 x S45cm (3 x 1½ft).

CULTIVATION It does best in a dry site, but is not always hardy.
COMBINATION Echinacea, Monarda, Potentilla, Sidalcea, Stipa

GERANIUM   CRANESBILL
Very useful filler plants that are invaluable for their attractive flowers and robust, ground-covering nature.

x oxonianum 'Rose Clair'

Satin-pink flowers fade to a soft pink and flower all summer long. Plants give good ground cover. H30 x S45cm (1 x 1½ft).

phaeum   DUSKY CRANESBILL, MOURNING WIDOW

Dark purple flowers appear in late spring, even in shade. H75 x S35cm (2½ x 1–1½ft).

phaeum 'Album'

Translucent, nodding white flowers appear in late spring on tall stems. This plant is suitable for deep shade and not-too-dry soil. H75 x S45cm (2½ x 1½ft).

phaeum 'Samobor'

Purple flowers open in late spring among leaves, strikingly marked with brown-black. H75 x S45cm (2½ x 1½ft).

psilostemon   ARMENIUM CRANESBILL
Cyclamen-red flowers with black hearts make an indescribably beautiful colour combination to be enjoyed for many weeks in midsummer. H90 x S75cm (3 x 2½ft).

sanguineum   BLOODY CRANESBILL
Lilac-red flowers open from early summer through to autumn. A rewarding, ground-cover plant that is more tolerant of dry places than most. H45 x S45cm (1½ x 1½ft).

soboliferum
Pink-lilac flowers appear in summer and the foliage develops good autumn colour. H30 x S20cm (1ft x 8in).

sylvaticum 'Amy Doncaster'
Deep blue flowers with a white heart produced in late spring. A healthy, good-looking plant that flowers twice. H60 x S30cm (2 x 1ft).

sylvaticum 'Baker's Pink'
With soft-pink flowers in late spring, it grows taller than 'Amy Doncaster' and has slightly larger leaves. H90 x S45cm (3 x 1½ft).

wlassovianum
Purple-lilac flowers succeed orange-red leaves that appear in early spring, and continue until the autumn. H35 x S30cm (1–1½ x 1ft).

HYBRID CULTIVARS
'Brookside'
Purple-blue flowers with a white heart appear from early to late summer. H45 x S30cm (1½ x 1ft).

'Dilys'
Red-purple flowers from midsummer to winter stud a cranesbill that gives good groundcover, and is useful for growing through other plants. H30 x S75cm (1 x 2½ft).

'Patricia'
Red flowers open for weeks in early summer. This hybrid has a good portion of *G. psilostemon* in its genes, but flowers for longer. The wide growth habit makes it suitable as groundcover for large spaces. H75 x S60cm (2½ x 2ft).

'Philippe Vapelle'
An abundance of blue flowers in early summer appears amid grey-green leaves. H45 x S45cm (1½ x 1½ft).

'Spinners'
Large, deep blue flowers open over many weeks from early summer. A good-looking, robust plant with a high proportion of *G. pratense*, of which it is very reminiscent. H75 x S45cm (2½ x 1½ft).

CULTIVATION Most species prefer sun but some will tolerate partial shade.

They tend to be happy in any soil as long as it is neither waterlogged nor dry for extended periods.
COMBINATIONS Amsonia, Aruncus, Astilbe, Digitalis, Gillenia, Hosta, Rodgersia.

GEUM AVENS
Small early summer-flowering perennials that make ideal filler plants.

rivale 'Leonard's Variety'
Nodding red flowers in early spring stand out well against the more pointed, velvety brown sepals within which they are housed. H30 x S30cm (1 x 1ft).

CULTIVATION Geums do best in full sun, and moist but well-drained soil.
COMBINATIONS Alchemilla, Asphodeline, Astrantia, Campanula, Iris, Nepeta, Stachys.

GILLENIA
These summer-flowering perennials are delicate and elegant. They can be used as filler plants, but also contribute structure on a small scale.

trifoliata BOWMAN'S ROOT, INDIAN PHYSIC
Little white flowers develop from small red buds on fine branches in midsummer. H90 x S60cm (3 x 2ft).

CULTIVATION Tolerant of sun or shade, gillenias thrive in any well-drained soil.
COMBINATIONS Astrantia, Astilbe, Euphorbia, Geranium, Geum, Salvia, Stachys.

GYPSOPHILA
Spring- and summer-flowering perennials with many tiny flowers, which makes them well suited to form screens and curtains.

altissima
Pale pink flowers appear in mid- to late summer on wide- and open-branched stems. H1.2m x S60cm (6 x 2ft).

CULTIVATION Grow them in full sun and deep, well-drained soil.
COMBINATIONS Achillea, Eryngium, Knautia, Lavandula, Monarda, Nepeta, Verbena, Veronicastrum.

HELENIUM SNEEZEWEED
Late summer- and autumn-flowering perennials that are grown for their sprays of daisy-like flowers.

'Die Blonde'
Small butter-yellow, daisy-like flowers with wide, fringed petals open in late summer. This is one of many good varieties. H1.5m x S60cm (5 x 2ft).

HYBRIDS
'Kupferzwerg'
Orange-red florets surround a darker heart. H1.2m x S60cm (4 x 2ft).

'Rubinzwerg'
Flowers are deep reddish-brown. H1.2m x S60cm (4 x 2ft).

CULTIVATION Heleniums require full sun and well-drained soil.
COMBINATIONS Aster, Calamagrostis, Echinacea, Eupatorium, Lobelia, Miscanthus, Persicaria, Sanguisorba, Selinum, Veronicastrum.

HELIANTHUS SUNFLOWER
Late summer- and autumn-flowering perennials that are grown for their large, daisy-like flowers.

salicifolius (SYN. H. ORGYALIS)
WILLOW-LEAVED SUNFLOWER
Small, yellow, daisy-like flowers open in autumn on stout, upright stems which carry many fine leaves. H2.5m x S90cm (8 x 3ft).

HYBRIDS
'Lemon Queen'
Soft yellow daisy-like flowers in late summer on plants that form huge clumps. H2m x S90cm (6½ x 3ft).

CULTIVATION Sunflowers prefer sun and well-drained soil.
COMBINATIONS Aster, Eupatorium, Helenium, Miscanthus, Perovskia, Phlox, Verbena, Veronicastrum.

HELLEBORUS HELLEBORE
Semi-evergreen perennials grown for their winter and spring flowers, although the leaves, too, can be quite striking. They make good fillers.

argutifolius (SYN. H. CORSICUS)
CORSICAN HELLEBORE
The Corsican hellebore's green-white flowers appear in large clusters in late winter. H45 x S75cm (1½ x 2½ft).

foetidus STINKING HELLEBORE
Striking, soft green flowers hang down from bracts of the same colour as early as the very beginning of winter. The leaves are dark green and superbly serrated. A short-lived plant but it self-seeds. H45 x S45cm (1½ x 1½ft).

ORIENTALIS HYBRIDS
Cup-shaped white, pink or purple flowers, some speckled, appear late in winter amid evergreen, dense and divided foliage. H35 x S30cm (1–1½ x 1ft).

CULTIVATION Hellebores prefer semi-shade and moisture-retentive but well-drained soil.
COMBINATIONS Crocus, Euphorbia, Lamium, Lunaria, Primula vulgaris, Pulmonaria.

HEMEROCALLIS DAYLILY
Lily-like flowers, each lasting for a day, are borne in succession. Linear leaves make these valuable texture plants, especially for repetitive pattern-making throughout the border.

altissima
Branched clusters of yellow flowers open in midsummer on a tall and slender plant. H1.5m x S45cm (5ft x 1½ft).

citrina
Lemon, fragrant flowers on long stems in early summer. H90 x S45cm (3 x 1½ft).

HYBRID CULTIVARS
'Corky'
Small-flowered selection with buds marked with red-brown on the outsides. The small yellow flowers are held well clear of the plant and appear in early summer. H90 x S45 cm (3 x 1½ft).

'Duke of Durham'
Rather strange, but attractive, rusty orange flowers open in early summer. H60 x S30cm (2 x 1ft).

'Gentle Shepherd'
The best of the whites, this daylily blooms in early summer and each flower has a yellow-green throat. H75 x S45cm (2½ x 1½ft).

'Green Flutter'
Attractive, small yellow-green flowers appear in early summer. H75 x S45cm (2½ x 1½ft).

'Little Grapette'

Unusual, small, dark blood-red flowers with a yellow-green throat open in early summer. H45 x S30cm (1½ x 1ft).

'Nugget'

Orange-yellow, not-fully-opening flowers appear in early summer on a robust plant. H75 x S45cm (2½ x 1½ft).

'Pardon Me'

Dark red flowers with yellow-green throats open in early summer. H60 x S45cm (2 x 1½ft).

'Princess Blue Eyes'

Lilac flowers with yellow-green throats open in early summer. H75 x S45cm (2½ x 1½ft).

CULTIVATION Daylilies require full sun and fertile soil.
COMBINATIONS Achillea, Astrantia, Campanula, Delphinium, Geranium, Lychnis, Lythrum, Salvia, Scabiosa. Most grasses.

HEUCHERA ALUM ROOT, CORAL BELLS

Evergreen, summer-flowering perennials make useful filler and texture plants. Leaves are usually interestingly textured and form large clumps to give good groundcover.

micrantha 'Purple Ace'

White flowers open in late spring, but the large, shiny leaves are especially attractive. H45 x S30cm (1½ x 1ft).

CULTIVATION These plants prefer to grow in semi-shade and a moisture-retentive, well-drained soil.
COMBINATIONS Astrantia, Dicentra, Digitalis, Euphorbia, Geum, Hosta, Rodgersia.

HOSTA PLANTAIN LILY

Perennials grown for their decorative foliage, hostas can form huge clumps and make excellent groundcover. They are useful for adding variation to the visual structure of a border, and for this purpose the pleated texture of *H. sieboldiana* and its hybrids is particularly fine.

plantaginea var. grandiflora

Strikingly large, fragrant, white flowers appear in late summer. Leaves are a lighter green than those of most hostas. H45 x S30cm (1½ x 1ft).

SIEBOLDIANA HYBRIDS
'Blue Angel'

Greyish-blue leaves form compact clumps. Attractive white flowers in summer are followed by seedheads that persist and have good winter structure. H90 x S45cm (3 x 1½ft).

'Blue Impression'

Attractive lilac flowers in midsummer and blue leaves that are medium to large. H45 x S30cm (1½ x 1ft).

CULTIVATION Most hostas prefer shade and a rich, moist but well-drained neutral soil.
COMBINATIONS Astrantia, Astilbe, Calamagrostis, Cimcifuga, Euphorbia, Geranium, Heuchera, Rodgersia, Sanguisorba.

IRIS

Upright, rhizomatous or bulbous perennials that are grown for their strap-like leaves and flowers. Seedheads persist through winter, and those of *I. ensata* are particularly fine.

chrysographes

Abundant black-purple flowers with a velvety sheen, but last only for a short time in early summer. H75 x S45cm (2½ x 1½ft).

CULTIVATION This iris requires full sun and fairly rich, well-drained soil.
COMBINATIONS Astilboides, Filipendula, Geranium, Heuchera, Hosta.

KNAUTIA

Summer-flowering perennials with button-like flowers.

macedonica

Dark Bordeaux red, globular flowers, from midsummer until autumn, are held above deeply divided leaves. H60 x S30cm (2 x 1ft).

CULTIVATION This species needs full sun to thrive but grows in any soil, and is even tolerant of dry soils.
COMBINATIONS Angelica, Achillea, Artemisia, Coreopsis, Deschampsia, Eryngium, Salvia, Selinum, Stipa, Thalictrum.

LAVATERA MALLOW

Large and distinctive disc flowers have a

---

delicate texture. Plants grow tall but have a weak shape so are best used as fillers.

cachemiriana

Remarkably robust, silky lilac-pink flowers open in midsummer on a semi-evergreen subshrub with downy, ivy-shaped green leaves. H1.5m x S90cm (5 x 3ft).

CULTIVATION Lavateras need full sun, but grow well in any soil.
COMBINATIONS Achillea, Centranthus, Monarda, Perovskia, Phlox, Selinum, Thalictrum, Verbena. Most grasses.

LEUZEA CENTAUROIDES

Lilac-pink flowerheads embraced by brown, papery bracts appear briefly in midsummer. Although the flowering period is short, plants remain ornamental long after the flowers are over. H1.2m x S45cm (4 x 1½ft).

CULTIVATION Knapweeds require sun, but are happy in even the poorest soil.
COMBINATIONS Achillea, Campanula, Geranium, Gillenia, Phlomis, Salvia.

LIGULARIA

Distinctive robust habit and bold foliage, which is often textured or coloured. The large daisy-like flowers are held sometimes in spires, sometimes in branched clusters.

veitchiana

Fluffy, branched flowerheads arranged in golden yellow trusses in late summer turn into decorative, downy seedheads. Broad, heart-shaped leaves make this a superb, solitary plant. H1.4m x S90cm (4½ x 3ft).

CULTIVATION This species grows best in sun, in moist, well-drained soil, and is fully hardy.
COMBINATIONS Achnatherum, Astilbe, Filipendula, Hemerocallis, Lythrum, Persicaria, Rodgersia, Sanguisorba. Umbellifers like peucedanum or selinum.

LIMONIUM SEA LAVENDER, STATICE

Summer- and autumn-flowering perennials with tiny flowers in small panicles, often so sparse that they act as screens or curtains. Sea lavenders are also useful as filler plants.

---

gmelinii

Airy, narrow flower trusses of lavender-blue open in midsummer on this robust species. H60 x S45cm (2 x 1½ft).

CULTIVATION Sea lavenders require full sun and well-drained soil.
COMBINATIONS Centranthus, Eryngium, Gaura, Nepeta, Origanum, Potentilla.

LOBELIA

Late summer and autumn flowering perennials with flowers in spires, often with vivid colours.

x gerardii 'Rosencavalier'

Good border plant with deep pink flowers. Underlips are divided into three. H1m x S30cm (3½ x 1½ft).

x gerardii 'Vedrariensis'

Superb purple, lilac or violet flowers held on tall stems above lance-shaped, deep green leaves. H90 x S45cm (3 x 1½ft).

siphilitica

Blue flowers entirely cover robust, unbranched stems. H90 x S45cm (3 x 1½ft).

siphilitica 'Alba'

White form of the above species. H90 x S45cm (3 x 1½ft)

HYBRID CULTIVARS
'Eulalia Berridge'

The flowers are a unique pink and raspberry red and combine well with other perennials. H90 x S45cm (3 x 1½ft).

'Tania'

The flowers are a refined, though striking, purple-red borne on slightly darker stems. H90 x S45cm (3 x 1½ft).

CULTIVATION Grow them in sun and a moist fertile soil. Hybrids and x geradiii types should be protected against freezing in regions with severe winter weather.
COMBINATIONS Echinacea, Eupatorium, Gaura, Helenium, Persicaria, Selinum.

LUNARIA

Early-flowering biennials and perennials that are grown for their attractove flowers and silvery seed pods.

rediviva PERENNIAL HONESTY
Small, pale lilac, sweetly scented flowers in early spring are followed by flat, shiny silver, oval fruits which decorate the plant for a long time. H75 x S30cm (2½ x 1ft).

CULTIVATION This species prefers partial shade and not too dry a position.
COMBINATIONS Aquilegia, Cardamine, Dicentra, Digitalis, Euphorbia, Heuchera, Lamium, Mertensia.

LYCHNIS
Disc shaped flowers arranged in umbels. Short-lived, they self sow readily and flower in early summer.

chalcedonica var. albiflora
White flowers sit in circular clusters at the top of stems. H1.4m x S30 cm (4½ x 1ft).

chalcedonica 'Carnea'
A deep pastel pink colour rarely seen amongst perennials. Can be used to creates some specific accents in the border. H1.4m x S30 cm (4½ x 1ft).

CULTIVATION Sun and most soils, including dry ones.
COMBINATIONS Astilbe, Astrantia, Cirsium, Delphinium, Deschampsia, Thalictrum.

LYTHRUM LOOSESTRIFE
Summer-flowering waterside plants that bear flowers in spires.

salicaria 'Blush'
Soft, pink flowers are carried on a robust and well-branched plant. H1.2m x S60cm (4 x 2ft).

salicaria 'Stichflamme'
The flowers are large and pink-red. H1.2m x S60cm (4 x 2ft).

salicaria 'Zigeunerblut'
The bright red-purple flowers are particularly striking. H1.2m x S60cm (4 x 2ft).

virgatum
Lilac flowers open on a slender and refined plant. H90 x S60cm (3 x 2ft).

CULTIVATION These all like full sun or semi-shade and will grow happily in any soil that does not dry out; they are even tolerant of waterlogging.

COMBINATIONS Achillea, Calamagrostis, Calamintha, Echinacea, Ligularia, Macleaya, Panicum, Persicaria, Phlox, Verbena, Veronicastrum.

MACLEAYA
Summer-flowering perennials with tiny flowers that are grown for their elegant and strongly structural appearance.

cordata PLUME POPPY, TREE CELANDINE
Cream flowers in summer hover above grey-green, deeply lobed leaves. H2.2m x S90cm (7 x 3ft).

CULTIVATION Likes sun and flourishes in soil that is well-drained but not too dry.
COMBINATIONS Calamagrostis, Echinops, Helianthus, Lavatera, Miscanthus, Verbena.

MONARDA BEEBALM, WILD BERGAMOT
Button or globe flowers are arranged in whorls and open in midsummer. The foliage is aromatic.

'Aquarius'
Pale purple-violet flowers are highly attractive. H1.2m x S45cm (4 x 1½ft).

'Balance'
A highly regarded cultivar with intense pink flowers that are surrounded by brown-pink bracts. H1.2m x S45cm (4 x 1½ft).

'Beauty of Cobham'
Bright pink flowers are surrounded by very striking red bracts. H1.2m x S45cm (4 x 1½ft).

'Cherokee'
Pink flowers in summer fade to green seedheads, which in turn fade to a magnificent brown. H1.5m x S45cm (5 x 1½ft).

'Comanche'
Intense pink flowers with red bracts are produced right through into late summer. H1.8m x S45cm (6 x 1½ft).

'Fishes'
Pale pink florets encircle the hearts, which tend towards lime green. H90 x S45cm (3 x 1½ft).

'Kardinal'
Lilac-purple flowers are unusual in

that later blooms appear from the heart of the first flowers in late summer. H1.2m x S45cm (4 x 1½ft).

'Mohawk'
Deep lilac-pink blooms are surrounded by dark bracts. H1.5m x S45cm (5 x 1½ft).

'Ou Charm'
The pale pink flowers of this perennial are supported by dark red bracts and stems. H75 x S45cm (2½ x 1½ft).

'Pawnee'
Pink-lilac flower clusters have green hearts and green bracts. H1.8m x S60cm (6 x 2ft).

'Purple Ann'
Dark purple-red flowers and matching bracts appear in summer. H1.2m x S45cm (4 x 1½ft).

'Scorpion'
Striking, bright violet blooms are surrounded by dark bracts. H1.4m x S45cm (4½ x 1½ft).

'Sioux'
Virtually white flowers have a hint of lilac and are supported by pale green bracts. H1.2m x 45cm (4 x 1½ft).

'Snow Queen'
White flowers with lilac hints are carried on a slender plant. H1.4m x S45cm (4½ x 1½ft).

'Squaw'
Bright red blooms in late summer on plants free of mildew make this a good replacement for the popular old cultivar 'Cambridge Scarlet'. H1.2m x S60cm (4 x 2ft).

'Talud'
Red-pink blooms are produced over a long period on plants free of mildew. H1.2m x S45cm (4 x 1½ft).

CULTIVATION Monardas require sun and moist soil, but do not tolerate waterlogging.
COMBINATIONS Achillea, Angelica, Echinops, Gaura, Lavatera, Lysimachia, Miscanthus, Molinia, Phlox, Selinum, Veronicastrum.

NEPETA CATMINT
Summer-flowering perennials with a low, sprawling habit make superb filler plants.

clarkei
Whorls of blue-lilac, white-lipped flowers succeed dark buds in early summer. These are short-lived plants but they self-seed. H45 x S30cm (1½ x 1ft).

govaniana
Pale yellow flowers cover the slender-branched upright form in midsummer. Leaves exude a lemon fragrance. H90 x S45cm (3 x 1½ft).

racemosa 'Walker's Low'
Pale blue flowers open in midsummer. This is a good as a border plant and one suitable for edging. H60 x S45cm (2 x 1½ft).

sibirica 'Souvenir d'André Chaudron'
Abundant purple-blue blossom covers a spreading plant in mid- to late summer. H90 x S45cm (3 x 1½ft).

CULTIVATION All catmints prefer sun and moist but well-drained soil.
COMBINATIONS Achillea, Centranthus, Coreopsis, Gypsophila, Monarda, Saponaria, Sidalcea.

ORIGANUM MARJORAM, OREGANO
Scented-leaved plants that flower in mid- to late summer. Use as filler plants but with a good long-lasting structural plant close to.

'Rosenkuppel'
Lilac-pink flowers, much favoured by butterflies, cover this vigorous plant. H45 x S45cm (1½ x 1½ft).

CULTIVATION Oreganos prefers sun and well-drained, alkaline soil.
COMBINATIONS Achillea, Astrantia, Diascia, Eryngium, Gaura, Perovskia, Salvia, Sesleria.

PENSTEMON
Filler plants that are characterized by tubular flowers in summer.

digitalis 'Husker Red'
White, slightly pinkish flowers open from mid- until late summer above dark leaves. H75 x S30cm (2½ x 1ft).

CULTIVATION Penstemons do best in full sun and fertile, well-drained soil.

COMBINATIONS Achillea, Astrantia, Eryngium, Nepeta, Perovskia, Stipa.

PEROVSKIA
An important source of colour in mid-to late summer.

abrotanoides 'Blue Spire'
An attractive plant with upright, grey-white felty stems and grey saw-toothed leaves. The tiny flowers are violet-blue and form narrow spikes giving a misty impression from a distance. H1.2 x S40cm (4 x 1ft).

CULTIVATION Perovskia require full sun and are successful on dry soils.
COMBINATIONS Echinacea, Digitalis, Helenium, Liatris, Monarda, Panicum, Stipa.

PERSICARIA   (SYN. POLYGONUM)
Robust perennials carrying flowers in spires or panicles.

amplexicaulis   BISTORT
Flowers open in narrow, tail-like spikes in mid- to late summer. Rounded shape means this is best regarded as a filler plant. H1.2 x S1.2m (4 x 4ft).

amplexicaulis 'Alba'
Countless small white flowers form narrow inflorescences on slender plants in mid-to late summer. H1.2 x S1.2m (4 x 4ft).

amplexicaulis 'Firedance'
Bright red flowers bloom from midsummer to autumn. The leaves are narrower and more pointed than those of 'Alba'. H1.2 x S1.2m (4 x 4ft).

amplexicaulis 'Rosea'
Lovely deep pink flowers open from mid-summer to autumn. H1.2 x S1.2m (4 x 4ft).

amplexicaulis 'Summer Dance'
Pink flower spikes from midsummer until they are nipped by the first frost. H1.2 x S1.2m (4 x 4ft).

campanulata
Abundant clusters of white blossom on branched stems turn reddish pink as nights grow colder. Does not like too dry soil. H90 x S90cm (3 x 3ft).

filiformis
Slender, red-pink flower spikes in midsummer on a plant with rather coarse leaves marked with dark patches. H75 x S45cm (2½ x 1½ft).

polymorpha
Superb, cream flower plumes in midsummer on this, the giant of polygonums. It is not rampant. H2.5 x S1.4m (8 x 4½ft).

CULTIVATION These thrive in damp but well-drained places, in sun or half-shade.
COMBINATIONS Calamagrostis, Echinacea, Eupatorium, Miscanthus, Molinia, Nepeta, Phlox, Scabiosa, Thalictrum, Veronicastrum.

PEUCEDANUM
Small flowers are arranged in umbels on tall, hollow stems.

verticillare
Umbels of white flowers appear in midsummer on a short-lived plant that will self-seed. H2m x S60cm (6½ x 2ft).

CULTIVATION This species tolerates sun but can also thrive in partial shade, and is happy in any soil.
COMBINATIONS Cimicifuga, Echinops, Filipendula, Miscanthus, Phlomis, Veronicastrum.

PHLOMIS
Evergreen, summer-flowering shrubs and perennials produce flowers in tightly packed globes. Those considered here below are herbaceous perennials rather than actual shrubs.

pungens (syn.P. taurica)
Lilac-blue flowers are grouped in whorls in summer on a robust border plant. H90 x S45cm (3 x 1½ft).

tuberosa 'Amazone'
Abundant whorls of lilac-pink, lipped blossoms are carried on very long, scarcely branched flower stalks in summer. H1.8m x S60cm (6 x 2ft).

CULTIVATION These are happiest in sun and well-drained soil.
COMBINATIONS Calamagrostis, Campanula, Cirsium, Delphinium, Echinops, Lychnis, Molinia, Papaver, Salvia, Veronicastrum.

PHLOX
Midsummer flowers, often scented, are produced in panicles of good size.

maculata 'Delta'
The mass of white flowers, each with a distinctive lilac eye, are in clear contrast to the attractive, dark green, narrow, oblong leaves. H90 x S45cm (3 x 1½ft).

paniculata (wild form)
Perennial phlox, summerphlox. The small, pale lilac-blue flowers are stunning. H1.4m x S45 cm (4½ x 1½ft).

paniculata var. alba
Relatively small white flowers have a trace of pink in early summer. H1.4m x S45cm (4½ x 1½ft).

PANICULATA HYBRIDS
'Blue Paradise'
Unusual ink-blue flowers look best in soft light. H1.2m x S45cm (4 x 1½ft).

'Lichtspiel'
The colour of the pale pink-lilac flowers intensifies as twilight falls. H1.2m x S45cm (4 x 1½ft).

'Rosa Pastell'
This has pink flowers which have a small, darker pink eye in the centre. H90 x S45cm (3 x 1½ft).

'Rosa Spier'
Large pink flowers fade to a paler shade and have a striking, dark pink eye. H75 x S45cm (2½ x 1½ft).

'Utopia'
This is a new pink-flowered hybrid. H1.8m x S45cm (6 x 1½ft).

CULTIVATION Phlox thrive in sun or partial shade and in fertile, well-drained, but moist soil.
COMBINATIONS Echinacea, Gaura, Gypsophila, Helenium, Monarda, Selinum, Thalictrum, Veronicastrum. The wild forms of phlox combine very well with Calamagrostis.

POTENTILLA   CINQUEFOIL
Genus of perennials and subshrubs grown primarily as filler plants and for their foliage and flattish, saucer-shaped flowers.

x hopwoodiana
Pastel-pink flowers with red hearts open from mid- to late summer. Let it climb up extra long stalks of other plants to a height sufficient to give a stunning display. H45 x S30cm (1½ x 1ft).

HYBRID CULTIVAR
'Etna'
Velvety red, single-flowers open from mid- to late summer on a plant with hairy, silvery leaves. H45 x S25cm (1½ft x 10in).

CULTIVATION Grow potentillas in full sun and well-drained soil.
COMBINATIONS Achillea, Amsonia, Artemisia, Centranthus, Eryngium.

RODGERSIA
Genus of summer-flowering, rhizomatous perennials invaluable for their large, bold and highly textured leaves and panicles, often plume-like, of pale flowers.

aesculifolia
Cream flowers in summer rise above leaves that are similar to those of horse chestnut. Plant alone or in large groups in a moisture-retentive soil. H90 x S75cm (3 x 2½ft).

pinnata 'Superba'
Bunches of little pink flowers in midsummer are succeeded by countless seed capsules that later turn brown-red. Bronze-coloured leaves are slightly shiny. H75 x S45cm (2½ x 1½ft).

CULTIVATION Plant in sun or semi-shade, in moist soil and shelter from strong winds.
COMBINATIONS Aconitum, Astilbe, Astrantia, Calamagrostis, Cimicifuga, Deschampsia, Geranium, Heuchera, Hosta.

RUDBECKIA   CONEFLOWER
The striking, daisy-like flowerheads are usually yellow and open in late summer.

fulgida var. sullivantii 'Goldsturm'
Flowers have horizontal petals and bud-like, nearly black flower hearts. H90 x S30cm (3 x 1ft).

maxima

Yellow petals surround dark flower cones on a plant with large, blue-green leaves. H1.5m x S 45cm (5 x 1½ft).

CULTIVATION Fully hardy plants that thrive in sun or partial shade, in well-drained or moist soil.
COMBINATIONS Aster, Eupatorium, Panicum, Persicaria, Veronicastrum.

SALVIA

Important fillers that form low, rounded shapes and are characterized by aromatic leaves. The spire-shaped flower clusters are persistent and strongly structural.

glutinosa

Pale yellow flowers with brown markings open in summer, remaining decorative long after fading. This species has hairy leaves and stems, and tolerates shade – unusual for a salvia. H90 x S45cm (3 x 1½ft).

nemorosa 'Amethyst'

A recent introduction that has lilac-pink flowers throughout summer and a bushy habit. H90 x S45cm (3 x 1½ft).

x sylvestris 'Blauhügel'

The only variety whose blooms come close to blue. They are produced throughout summer. H45 x S30cm (1½ x 1ft).

x sylvestris 'Mainacht'

Small purple blooms surround the stems to form spikes. Flowers first open as early as late spring and continue throughout the summer. This variety is somewhat coarser than 'Blauhügel'. H45 x S30cm (1½ x 1ft).

x sylvestris 'Rügen'

A compact plant with purple-blue flowers that appear earlier than most salvia blossom. H30 x S30cm (1 x 1ft).

x sylvestris 'Schneehügel'

White flowers open in midsummer. H45 x S30cm (1½ x 1ft).

x sylvestris 'Tänzerin'

The little, purple-blue flowers in mid- to late summer are surrounded by attractively coloured bracts, which remain long after the petals have been shed. H75 x S30cm (2½ x 1ft).

sclarea CLARY

Lilac flowers with stunning lilac-pink bracts are produced in midsummer. This is short-lived, but usually self-seeds. H90 x S45cm (3 x 1½ft).

verticillata 'Purple Rain'

Small blue-lilac blooms nestle in whorls of purple-mauve sepals from midsummer to autumn. H45 x S30cm (1½ x 1ft).

verticillata 'Smouldering Torches'

Similar to 'Purple Rain', but more upright, with deeper coloured stems and bracts.

HYBRID CULTIVARS

'Dear Anja'

Abundant white-lipped, lilac flowers in summer have dark stalks and sepals. H60 x S25 cm (2ft x 10in).

CULTIVATION Salivas like sun and fertile, well-drained soil.
COMBINATIONS Achillea, Centranthus, Delphinium, Eryngium, Festuca, Filipendula, Geranium, Geum, Lychnis, Origanum, Stipa, Thalictrum.

SANGUISORBA

Elegant pinnate leaves and button-like flowers, which are held in large, bottlebrush-like clusters and widely dispersed enough to form see-through screens.

canadensis CANADIAN BURNET

White flowers are carried in long spikes in late summer on a robust, upright plant. H1.5m x S60cm (5 x 2ft).

officinalis GREAT BURNET, BURNET BLOODWORT

Abundant red flowers in summer adorn a slender plant with many branches. H1.4m x S60cm (4½ x 2ft).

officinalis 'Tanna'

Bright red flowers in summer on a plant that grows shorter than S. officinalis. H75 x S45cm (2½ x 1½ft).

tenuifolia 'Alba'

In late summer white flowerheads are carried atop long, overhanging stems,

resembling little elephants' trunks. The plant takes on attractive autumn colouring. H1.8m x S60cm (6 x 2ft).

tenuifolia 'Purpurea'

Red-flowered variety has a stiffer habit than 'Alba'. H1.5m x S60cm (5 x 2ft).

CULTIVATION Sun and moist soil are the main requirements.
COMBINATIONS Astilbe, Delphinium, Echinacea, Filipendula, Helenium, Hemerocallis, Thalictrum. All garden umbellifers.

SAPONARIA SOAPWORT

These summer-flowering perennials with good-sized flowers are best used as filler plants.

x lempergii 'Max Frei'

Produces pink blooms over a long period in late summer. H45 x S20cm (1½ft x 8in).

CULTIVATION Need sun and well-drained soil.
COMBINATIONS Lavandula, Monarda, Origanum, Perovskia, Scabiosa, Veronica.

SCABIOSA PINCUSHION FLOWER, SCABIOUS

Button-shaped flowerheads on long stalks are produced in summer.

japonica var. alpina

Lilac-blue flowers open from early summer on a low-growing, problem-free plant. H35 x S20cm (1–1½ft x 8in).

CULTIVATION Scabious prefers sun and well-drained, alkaline soil.
COMBINATIONS Achillea, Geranium, Monarda, Nepeta, Panicum, Salvia, Sporobolus, Verbena.

SCUTELLARIA HELMET FLOWER, SKULLCAP

These perennials are grown for their spires of distinctive tubular flowers.

incana

Spiky, blue flowers in late summer are still attractive when faded. The leaves are felty and grey. H60 x S25cm (2ft x 10in).

CULTIVATION Sun and well-drained soil are the main requirements.
COMBINATIONS Aster, Calamintha, Echinacea, Persicaria, Selinum, Serratula, Tricyrtis.

SEDUM STONECROP

Fleshy, succulent perennials with overall shape that is low and compact make good filler plants. The flowers are tightly clustered in heads and followed by persistent seed-heads which are potentially important for winter structure.

telephium subsp. maximum

Yellow flower clusters appear from late summer and last until autumn with grey leaves, which emerge from purple buds on purple stems. These combine to give this plant a striking appearance. H45 x S45cm (1½ x 1½ft).

telephium subsp. ruprechtii

Bright yellow flower clusters appear from late summer to autumn on this, not the most robust of sedums. H45 x S45cm (1½ x 1½ft).

HYBRID CULTIVARS

'Bertram Anderson'

Small red flowers and purple-red leaves make this low-growing sedum excellent for groundcover in the late summer season. H25 x S35cm (10in x 1–1½ft).

telephium 'Matrona'

Pink flowers, opening from late summer to autumn, red stalks and grey-green leaves together form a upright, tall and robust sedum. H75 x S60cm (2½ x 2ft).

telephium 'Munstead Red'

Flowerheads turn a splendid reddy brown in autumn. The grey-green leaves have red stalks. H45 x S45cm (1½ x 1½ft).

'Purple Emperor'

Red-brown flowers from late summer to autumn contrast strongly with the near-black leaves. H45 x S30cm (1½ x 1ft).

spectabile 'Stardust'

Broad and flat flowerheads of off-white open from late summer to early autumn. H45 x S30cm (1½ x 1ft).

CULTIVATION Sedums need sun and fertile, well-drained soil.
COMBINATIONS Achillea, Geranium, Nepeta, Panicum, Salvia, Stachys.

SELINUM

Genus of summer-flowering perennials that produce flowerheads in umbels.

wallichianum

Small white flowers clustered in umbels appear above a canopy of fine, lace-like leaves from later summer to early autumn. H90 x S45cm (3 x 1½ft).

CULTIVATION Short-lived plants that grow in sun or semi-shade, in any well-drained soil. They resent disturbance to roots.
COMBINATIONS Aconitum, Echinacea, Eupatorium, Filipendula, Knautia, Lysimachia, Phlox, Scabiosa, Thalictrum.

SERRATULA

Thistle-like daisy flowerheads appear in autumn. These are filler plants that also look good in winter.

seoanei

Abundant lilac-pink blooms from late summer remain decorative throughout the winter until the following spring. Plants are reminiscent of a small aster. H30 x S20cm (1ft x 8in).

CULTIVATION These plants require sun and well-drained soil.
COMBINATIONS Achillea, Euphorbia, Origanum, Sedum.

SIDALCEA   CHECKER MALLOW, PRAIRIE MALLOW

These summer-flowering perennials are grown for their small, hollyhock-like, disc-shaped blooms.

'My Love'

Expressive pink flowers open from midsummer and last until early autumn. H90 x S45cm (3 x 1½ft).

CULTIVATION Checker mallows require sun to thrive but are happy in any type of well-drained soil.
COMBINATIONS Achillea, Anthemis, Calamintha, Echinacea, Echinops, Monarda, Panicum, Phlox, Scabiosa, Veronica.

SOLIDAGO   GOLDEN ROD

Late-summer- and autumn-flowering perennials noted for their yellow plume-like flowerheads.

'Golden Mosa'

Sprays of mimosa-like yellow flowerheads appear above yellowish-green leaves. H75 x S60cm (2½ x 2ft).

rugosa 'Golden Rain'

Spreading, yellow inflorescences form on an upright plant which has dark stems. It is suitable for less cultivated parts of the garden. H1.2m x S75cm (4 x 2½ft).

CULTIVATION Golden rods are tolerant of sun or shade and any soil type.
COMBINATIONS Anemone, Calamagrostis, Cimicifuga, Helenium, Helianthus, Miscanthus, Scutellaria, Stipa, Verbena.

STACHYS   BETONY, HEDGE NETTLE, WOUNDWORT

Late spring- or summer-flowering plants that make good fillers.

byzantina 'Big Ears'

A form of lamb's ears or lamb's tongue primarily grown for its large and grey downy leaves which appear in the spring. The foliage combines with both gaudy colours and softer tones, but looks uninteresting in winter. H45 x S45cm (1½ x 1½ft).

macrantha 'Superba'

Attractive lilac-pink flowers are grouped in whorls around the stems from early summer. Ribbed leaves have serrated edges. H75 x S45cm (2½ x 1½ft).

monieri 'Hummelo'

Lilac flower spikes in early summer are much favoured by bees. Faded blooms remain attractive until late autumn. H90 x S45cm (3 x 1½ft).

officinalis 'Rosea'

Pale pink flowers form spikes on tall stalks in early summer. H90 x S45cm (3 x 1½ft).

CULTIVATION An open, sunny position is preferred and any well-drained soil, even one that is very poor.
COMBINATIONS Amsonia, Deschampsia, Hemerocallis, Salvia.

TEUCRIUM   GERMANDER, WOOD SAGE

Perennials that bear flowers in spires and with aromatic foliage.

hircanicum

Elegant, purple-pink flower spikes appear from midsummer until autumn. H45 x S30cm (1½ x 1ft).

CULTIVATION This germander requires full sun but grows well in any well-drained soil.
COMBINATIONS Diascia, Gaura, Nepeta, Origanum, Stachys, Stipa, Veronicastrum.

THALICTRUM   MEADOW RUE

Fluffy, sparse flowerheads, divided foliage and an upright habit combine to provide a useful screen or curtain.

aquilegifolium var. album

White, fluffy flowers borne on striking, dark purple stems in summer. H90 x S45cm (3 x 1½ft).

aquilegifolium 'Purpureum'

Fluffy, feathery, branched clusters of strong lilac-pink flowers appear in early summer. H1.2m x S45cm (4 x 1½ft).

delavayi

Large, airy, branched clusters of lilac flowers with yellow stamens are produced from mid- to late summer. H1.4m x S25cm (4½ft x 10in).

lucidum

Plumes of little, pale yellow flowers appear in summer on robust stalks, branched at the top. H2m x S75cm (6½ x 2½ft).

polygamum

Fresh white flowers in summer are borne on stems so robust that they remain standing right through the winter until the following spring, providing a splendid winter silhouette. H1.8m x S45cm (6 x 1½ft).

rochebruneanum

In early summer small lilac flowers with yellow stamens are ranged in airy, loosely branched clusters. The flowerheads combine together with striking red-brown stalks to form an impressive plant. H1.8m x S45cm (6 x 1½ft).

CULTIVATION Sun or light shade and well-drained soil are the main requirements for these perennials.
COMBINATIONS Aconitum, Echinacea, Eryngium, Filipendula, Monarda, Phlomis, Phlox, Sanguisorba, Sidalcea, Veronicastrum.

VERATRUM

Powerful structure plant that carries its flowers in branched spires and has impressive, pleated foliage.

californicum

This elegant veratrum flowers in midsummer. Its greenish yellow stamens contrast against dark centres. H2m x S50cm (6½ft x 2ft)

nigrum

Abundance of small mahogany-coloured flowers almost entirely cover the long, slender stems in late summer. Broad, oval leaves are neatly pleated. H1.2m x S35cm (4 x 1–1½ft).

CULTIVATION Requires semi-shade and fertile, moist soil.
COMBINATIONS Calamagrostis, Cimicifuga, Eupatorium, Persicaria, Peucedanum, Sanguisorba, Selinum.

VERBASCUM   MULLEIN

Short-lived summer-flowering perennials and biennials that bear their flowers in spires, which are sometimes branched.

chaixii 'Album'
WHITE NETTLE-LEAVED MULLEIN

Small creamy white flowers in midsummer open amid grey, hairy leaves. Faded plants have an attractive winter silhouette. H1.4m x S45cm (4½ x 1½ft).

CULTIVATION Mulleins prefer well-drained soil and a sunny, open site, but they will also tolerate some shade.
COMBINATIONS Achillea, Echinops, Gypsophila, Helenium, Monarda, Perovskia, Sanguisorba. Most grasses.

VERBENA   VERVAIN

Summer- and autumn-flowering perennials with numerous tiny flowers which are generally borne in spires. These perennials are much favoured by butterflies.

bonariensis

This has purple flowers from summer through to autumn and is one of the best curtain plants, with an open-branched, transparent quality.

hastata

Small purple-blue flowers appear in late summer on strong stems, branched like a candelabra. The leaves are narrow and pointed. H1.2m x S30cm (4 x 1ft).

CULTIVATION Verbenas prefer sun and any well-drained soil.
COMBINATIONS Artemisia, Echinacea, Eupatorium, Monarda, Molinia, Panicum, Perovskia, Phlox, Sanguisorba, Veronicastrum.

VERBESINA   CROWN BEARD
These are tall prairie perennials with pretty daisy flowers.

alternifolia   WINGSTEM, YELLOW IRONWEED
Yellow flowers are grouped in feathery heads in late summer and rough, lancet-like leaves. H2m x S45cm (6½ x 1½ft).

CULTIVATION Give this species a sunny, dry position.
COMBINATIONS Aster, Foeniculum, Persicaria, Perovskia.

VERNONIA   IRONWEED
Tall prairie perennials of the daisy family with flowers grouped in flat heads.

crinita 'Mammuth'
Lilac-purple flowers, reminiscent of asters, open in late summer on stems that are branched at the top. This is a tall, robust plant. H2.2m x S30cm (7 x 1ft).

CULTIVATION Ironweeds require sun but they will grow happily in any well-drained soil.
COMBINATIONS Aster, Eupatorium, Helenium, Miscanthus, Solidago

VERONICA   BIRD'S EYE, SPEEDWELL
These bear spires of flowers, usually blue.

'Inspiration'
Tall, white flower spikes in mid- to late summer provide excellent height in a border. H75 x S30cm (2½ x 1ft).

'Pink Damask'
Susceptible to mildew, but in moist soil it will produce long, pink spikes of flowers in mid- to late summer. H75 x S25 cm (2½ ft x 8in).

CULTIVATION Sun and well-drained soil.
COMBINATIONS Achillea, Artemisia, Calamagrostis, Echinacea, Gaura, Helenium, Panicum, Phlomis, Phlox, Stipa.

spicata 'Spitzentraum'
Blue flowers, from mid to late summer, harmonize well with striking grey-green leaves. H45 x S30cm (1½ x 1ft).

VERONICASTRUM
Blackroot, bowman's root, Culver's root Distinctive perennials with tiny flowers packed into narrow spires.

virginicum 'Apollo'
Very robust, lilac flowerheads, some 30cm (1ft) long, formed on slightly twisted stems in midsummmer. H1.8m x S45cm (6 x 1½ft).

virginicum 'Diana'
Spikes of white flowers in midsummer are carried on robust, upright stems. H1.4m x S35cm (4½ x 1–1½ft).

virginicum 'Fascination'
Striking lilac flowers twist up tall stems in midsummer. H1.8m x S45cm (6 x 1½ft).

virginicum var. incarnatum
(SYN. VAR. ROSEUM)
Pink flowers in midsummer fade to contribute their winter silhouette. H1.4m x S45cm (4½ x 1½ft).

virginicum 'Lavendelturm'
Subtle, pale-lilac flowers open in midsummer. H1.4m x S45cm (4½ x 1½ft).

virginicum 'Temptation'
Small blue flowers are borne on robust, upright branches in midsummer. Its narrowly lance-shaped leaves are arranged in whorls. H1.4m x S30cm (4½ x 1ft).

VIOLA   PANSY, VIOLET
Use as filler plants and enjoy the attractive small flowers.

cornuta   HORNED VIOLET,
Splendid purple-blue flowers open in late spring. H25 x S20cm (10 x 8in).

CORNUTA HYBRID
'Belmont Blue'
Pale blue flowers produced on a twisting stem from spring to autumn without interruption. H25 x S25cm (10 x 10in).

elatior
Pale blue flowers with white, veined hearts appear from midsummer till autumn

between long and slender horizontal leaves. H25 x S10cm (10 x 4in).

CULTIVATION Violets prefer semi-shade and moist soil.
COMBINATIONS Achillea, Anthemis, Geum, Heuchera, Lamium, Salvia, Saponaria.

ornamental grasses

CALAMAGROSTIS
Characterized by plume-like inflorescences that tower above the foliage in late summer and persist through winter. These often produce imposing plumes or spires of spikelet flowers.

x acutiflora 'Karl Foerster'
Flowers first appear in early summer but the faded inflorescences on stiff upright stems, remain until the following spring. Best used as a solitary grass. H1.8m x S45cm (6 x 1½ft).

brachytricha
(SYN. CALAMAGROSTIS BRACHYTRYCHA)
A good solitary, ornamental grass with feathery plumes. H1.2m x S60cm (4 x 2ft).

CULTIVATION Reed grasses do best in full sun, but tolerate dry or wet soil.
COMBINATIONS Echinacea, Eupatorium, Lavatera, Lobelia, Monarda, Persicaria, Phlomis, Phlox, Rudbeckia, Sanguisorba, Verbascum, Veronicastrum. Garden umbellifers.

CAREX   SEDGE
Filler plants with textured grass-like foliage.

muskingumensis   PALM BRANCH SEDGE
This sedge is reminiscent of papyrus with insignificant flowers in midsummer and semi- evergreen lancet-shaped leaves ranged around the stalks. H60 x S60cm (2 x 2ft).

CULTIVATION An easy-going sedge that likes sun or partial shade and happy in any soil.
COMBINATIONS Aster, Calamagrostis, Cimicifuga, Campanula, Geranium, Hosta, Persicaria, Rodgersia, Salvia.

DESCHAMPSIA   HAIR GRASS
Filler plants whose foliage, flowers and seedheads are useful for providing texture.

cespitosa 'Goldschleier'
Golden yellow flowerheads form in midsummer on this evergreen grass. H1.2m x S75cm (4 x 2½ft).

cespitosa 'Goldtau'
Soft golden flowers in midsummer adorn this small compact form of the evergreen tufted hair grass. H75 x S45cm (2½ x 1½ft).

CULTIVATION These like sun or partial shade and any soil; they are especially tolerant of moist ground.
COMBINATIONS Astrantia, Campanula, Hosta, Lobelia, Persicaria, Rodgersia.

HAKONECHLOA
Filler plants that are a useful source of foliage texture.

macra
Forms thick tufts with long, overhanging leaves which turn a splendid orange-yellow in autumn. H30 x S45cm (1 x 1½ft).

CULTIVATION Happy in sun or partial shade these grasses require good moist soil.
COMBINATIONS Aster, Ceratostigma, Persicaria, Scutellaria.

LUZULA   WOODRUSH
Filler plants whose foliage is useful for texture.

luzuloides 'Schneehäschen'
White flowers in early summer open above the splendid, narrow, silver-haired leaves. H75 x S45cm (2½ x 1½ft).

sylvatica 'Wäldler'
Clusters of white flowers appear in midsummer among narrow, evergreen leaves. This is a clump-forming and spreading plant. H35 x S30cm (1–1½ x 1ft).

CULTIVATION Woodrushes require sun or shade and humus-rich soil. They will tolerate dry conditions once established.
COMBINATIONS Euphorbia, Geranium, Hemerocallis, Heuchera, Hosta, Pulmonaria, Rodgersia.

MISCANTHUS

Essentially structural plants bearing large flowerheads in spires and plumes.

sinensis

Stunning ornamental grasses with strong winter silhouettes, as most cultivated varieties manage to remain upright all winter. There are many beautiful and varying forms in cultivation. H2.7 x S1.2m (9 x 4ft).

SINENSIS CULTIVARS

'Flamingo'

Silver-pink inflorescences appear from late summer to autumn on a robust, upright plant. H2m x S60cm (6½ x 2ft).

'Flammenmeer'

This cultivar has rich red autumn colouring and is very robust. H1.5m x S60cm (5 x 2ft).

'Gracillimus' MAIDEN GRASS

This is a non-flowering miscanthus chosen for its fine, narrow leaves. A few mature specimen plants can define the entire tone of the garden. H1.8m x S90cm (6 x 3ft).

'Graziella'

Flowerheads hang free above the foliage. They are initially reddish-silver but turn pure silver in late summer to autumn. One of the few grasses unsuited to heavy soils. H1.8m x S75cm (6 x 2½ft).

'Kleine Silberspinne'

Abundant silver-red inflorescences, held well clear of the leaves, appear in late summer and early autumn. The leaves are very fine and white-veined. H1.5m x 90cm (5 x 3ft).

'Malepartus'

Superb as the golden-brown, ribbed flower stems and inflorescences open in late summer. H2m x S90cm (6½ x 3ft).

'Morning Light'

Silvery grey-green leaves are reminiscent of *M. gracillimus*. H1.5m x S90cm (5 x 3ft).

'Pünktchen'

Loose brown flowerheads in early autumn add their beauty to the golden-yellow striped leaves. H2m x S90cm (6½ x 3ft).

'Roland'

Drooping inflorescences remain silver-white

well into winter on this grass of tall, loose form. H2.5 x S1.2m (8 x 4ft).

'Samurai'

Erect, brown-red inflorescences in early autumn turn silver later on. Leaves take on yellow tints in autumn on this upright, robust grass. H2m x S75cm (6½ x 2½ft).

'Silberspinne'

Erect brownish plumes in autumn and narrow leaves that remain green for a long time. H2m x S90cm (6½ x 3ft).

'Silberturm'

The elegant cream inflorescences in early autumn are held well above the leaves and persist to give an attractive winter silhouette. H2.5m x S90cm (8 x 3ft).

CULTIVATION Full sun and any soil; they take about three years to become established.
COMBINATIONS Aster, Eupatorium, Helenium, Persicaria, Phlomis, Veronicastrum.

MOLINIA

Essential grasses for structure, but their texture is fine enough to form a good screen.

caerulea subs. caerulea 'Edith Dudszus'

A dark, slender form of the purple moor grass with slightly overhanging inflorescences from midsummer to autumn held on robust stems. H90 x S45cm (3 x 1½ft).

caerula subs. arundinacea 'Karl Foerster'

Stiff, upright grass with a dark and open inflorescence, looking superb in autumn but does not remain standing in winter. H2.2m x 75cm (7 x 2½ft).

caerulea subs. caerulea 'Overdam'

Short, robust stems and fine leaves make up a tufted grass that looks a little like a hedgehog! H60 x S30cm (2 x 1ft).

caerula subs. arundinacea 'Transparent'

Open flowerheads give an impression of lightness, but this robust grass can be effective in borders. H2.2m x S90cm (7 x 3ft).

CULTIVATION These grasses thrive in any moist soil.

COMBINATIONS Cimicifuga, Echinacea, Eupatorium, Lobelia, Monarda, Persicaria, Salvia, Sedum, Selinum, Veronicastrum.

PANICUM   CRAB GRASS, PANIC GRASS

The fine flowerheads make panicums useful plants for providing screens and curtains in the garden.

virgatum 'Heavy Metal'

An attractive grass with typical panicum inflorescences in midsummer. The switch-like flowerheads bestow an impression of lightness on a rather stiff plant with grey-blue leaves. H1.2m x S45cm (4 x 1½ft).

virgatum 'Rehbraun'

The airy inflorescences in summer make delightful bouquets; in autumn the leaves turn red-brown. H1.2m x S60cm (4 x 2ft).

CULTIVATION Full sun and any soil as long as there is some moisture.
COMBINATIONS Achillea, Echinacea, Helenium, Lavatera, Lobelia, Perovskia, Rudbeckia, Sedum, Verbena.

SESLERIA   MOOR GRASS

Filler plants with good textural foliage.

autumnalis

Fresh green straw-coloured flowers appear in late summer. Evergreen plants that like shade. H50cm (2ft).

nitida   NEST MOOR GRASS

Grey-white flowers appear from among fairly stiff, metallic-grey leaves in spring. This grass looks attractive alongside other grey-leaved plants. H45 x S45cm (1½ x 1½ft).

CULTIVATION Require sun and average soil.
COMBINATIONS Achillea, Astrantia, Geranium, Platycodon, Polemonium, Potentilla.

SPODIOPOGON

A small genus of grasses characterized by spire-like flower- and seedheads.

sibiricus

Red-brown, narrow flowerheads in late summer develop a stronger colour in autumn. The leaves are rather bamboo-like and form a plant suitable not only for solitary use, but also as a low, dividing screen. H1.2m x S45cm (4 x 1½ft).

CULTIVATION Sun or partial shade, in moist soil, although it will tolerate dry conditions.
COMBINATIONS Aster, Aconitum, Echinacea, Persicaria, Sanguisorba.

SPOROBOLUS   DROPSEED, RUSH GRASS

Fine flower- and seedheads make these grasses ideal for a low screen.

heterolepis

Long, elegant, scented flowerheads held above waving fine, bright green leaves from midsummer until autumn. H75 x S35cm (2½ x 1–1½ft).

CULTIVATION Full sun and dry, stony soil are the essential requirements.
COMBINATIONS Aster, Echinacea, Geranium, Helenium, Knautia, Rudbeckia, Scabiosa, Verbena.

STIPA

Feather grass, needle, grass, spear grass. Most feather grasses possess fine flower- and seedheads which form screens or curtains.

calamagrostis

A splendid, tuft-forming grass with long stalks of overhanging, loose, feathery plumes that emerge in early summer and remain attractive until late winter. H90 x S45cm (3 x 1½ft).

gigantea

Tuft-forming grass with slender grey-green leaves and particularly decorative flower-heads in early summer, resembling oats, on tall stems. H2.2m x S90cm (7 x 3ft).

pulcherrima

Improbably long silver 'tails' appear in early summer and quiver in the slightest breeze above the grey leaves. This grass is short-lived. H1.2m x S45cm (4 x 1½ft).

turkestanica

The elegant stalks, blue-green leaves and upright form of this grass combine well with colourful perennials. H75 x S35cm (2½ x 1–1½ft).

CULTIVATION Feather grasses thrive in full sun and any garden soil.
COMBINATIONS Amsonia, Achillea, Artemisia, Eryngium, Origanum, Papaver, Salvia.

index

Page numbers in *italics* refer to illustrations. Page numbers in **bold** refer to the plant directory.

authors' acknowledgments

I could not have achieved what I have done without the support of many other people, first and foremost my wife Anja, who is always right behind me in everything I do. Henk Gerritsen, a kindred spirit in his love of wild plants, has been a valued colleague, with whom I have worked on more than one book. Rob Leopold has also been a constant friend since the early days of the 'perennial movement', whilst nurseryman Ernst Pagels in Leer, Germany, has been a mentor and the source of some of my best plants.

I'm very grateful to my clients over the years, without whom it would have been impossible to develop my garden style, in particular to Saskia and Fezie Khaleghi, John Coke and Familie van Steeg, whose gardens are featured here, and to Stefan Mattson, in Enköping, Sweden, who commissioned a major park planting. I also owe a lot to Aad and Joke Zoet, and to Aad and El Geerlings, fellow growers whose support in large-scale growing has enabled me to undertake many exciting projects.

Piet Oudolf

I've known Piet and Anja Oudolf for some years now, and have always immensely enjoyed their friendship and hospitality, out of which this book grew.

I'm grateful to various other mutual colleagues with whom I've discussed Piet's work: John Coke in Farnham, England, Michael King in Amsterdam, Rob Leopold in Groningen, Uschi Gräfen in Freising, Germany, and Sabine Plenk in Vienna. I'm especially grateful to Eva Gustavsson in Alnarp, Sweden, for reading through the Introduction and making some valuable comments, and to my partner Jo Elliot, for her ceaseless love and support.

The editorial staff at Conran Octopus have worked hard to produce an exciting book, our thanks go to them, to photographer Nicola Browne, and also to Fiona Lindsay, our agent, whose unique combination of charm and terrier-like tenacity was a vital part in securing a contract.

Noël Kingsbury

publisher's acknowledgments

The Publisher would like to thank the following photographers and organizations for permission to reproduce their work.

1–2 Piet Oudolf; **3** *left* Nicola Browne; **3** *centre & right* Piet Oudolf; **4** *left* Piet Oudolf; **4** *centre & right* Nicola Browne; **6** *left* Noel Kingsbury (Designers: Grafen/Muhler, Klenzepark, Ingolstadt); **6** *right* Andrew Lawson (Waterperry Gardens, Oxon); **7** *left* Marcus Harpur ('Barnards', Essex); **7** *right* Piet Oudolf; **8** *left* John Neubauer/The Garden Picture Library; **8** *right* Noel Kingsbury; **9** *left* Frank Oberle; **9** *right* Piet Oudolf; **10** Marijke Heuff (Mien Ruys, Dedemsvaart, Holland); **11** Marijke Heuff; **12–13** Noel Kingsbury; **14** *left* Piet Oudolf; **14–16** Nicola Browne; **16** *centre left* Piet Oudolf: **17** *left, centre right right & right* Nicola Browne; **17** *centre left left, centre left & centre right* Piet Oudolf; **18** Piet Oudolf; **18** *above centre* Nicola Browne; **19** Piet Oudolf; **20** *left* Nicola Browne; **20** Piet Oudolf; **21** Piet Oudolf; **21** *below right* Marijke Heuff; **22–23** Piet Oudolf; **24** *left, above centre & below centre* Nicola Browne; **24** *above, centre & below* Piet Oudolf; **25** Piet Oudolf; **26** *left, above centre & below* Piet Oudolf; **26** *above & below centre* Nicola Browne; **27** *above & below centre* Piet Oudolf; **27** *above centre & below* Nicola Browne; **28** left Nicola Browne; **28** Piet Oudolf; **29** Piet Oudolf; **30** *left & below right* Piet Oudolf; **30** *top right* Nicola Browne **31** *top left* Nicola Browne; **31** *top right, below left & below right* Piet Oudolf; **32-36** Piet Oudolf; **37** Piet Oudolf; **37** *below right* Nicola Browne; **38** *above left* Nicola Browne; **38** Piet Oudolf; **39** Piet Oudolf; **40–41** Nicola Browne; **42** Piet Oudolf; **42** *centre right* Nicola Browne; **43** *left & centre left* Piet Oudolf; **43** *centre right & right* Nicola Browne; **44** Nicola Browne; **45** Piet Oudolf; **46** *above* Piet Oudolf; **46** *below* Nicola Browne; **47** Piet Oudolf; **48** Piet Oudolf; **48** *below* Nicola Browne; **50** Nicola Browne; **51** Piet Oudolf; **51** *right* Stefan Mattson; **52–53** Piet Oudolf; **54–59** Nicola Browne; **60** Piet Oudolf; **61** Nicola Browne; **62** *above* Nicola Browne; **62** *below* Marijke Heuff; **62–63** *centre* Piet Oudolf; **63** Nicola Browne; **64** Piet Oudolf; **65–67** Nicola Browne; **69** *above* Marijke Heuff; **69** *below* Piet Oudolf; **70** Marijke Heuff; **70–71** Piet Oudolf; **71** Marijke Heuff; **72–73** Piet Oudolf; **74** Nicola Browne; **75–77** Piet Oudolf; **78** *left* Nicola Browne; **78–79** Piet Oudolf; **80** *left* Piet Oudolf; **80** *right* Marijke Heuff; **81–82** Nicola Browne; **83–84** Piet Oudolf; **85–86** Nicola Browne; **87–88** Piet Oudolf; **91** *above* Piet Oudolf; **91** *below* Nicola Browne; **92–93** Piet Oudolf; **94** *left & centre* Piet Oudolf; **94** *right* Nicola Browne; **95** *left & right* Nicola Browne; **95** centre Marijke Heuff; **96–99** Piet Oudolf; **100–101** Nicola Browne; **102–106** Piet Oudolf; **107** Nicola Browne; **108–109** Piet Oudolf; **110–111** Stefan Mattson; **112** Piet Oudolf; **113** Anders Forngren; **114–122** Piet Oudolf; **122–123** Nicola Browne; **123** Piet Oudolf; **124** *left & right* Piet Oudolf; **124** *centre* Nicola Browne; **125–134**; **135** Nicola Browne; **136** *above* Marijke Heuff; **136** *below* Piet Oudolf; **137–138** Piet Oudolf; **139** *above* Marijke Heuff; **139** *below* Piet Oudolf; **140–143** Piet Oudolf.

All photographs by Nicola Browne specially commissioned by Conran Octopus.